# "Is This Going to Be on the Test?"

## and Ten Other Questions That Can Save Your College Career

### THIRD EDITION

**Randall E. Majors**

*Revision Author*
**Joan Marie Yamasaki**

**GORSUCH SCARISBRICK, PUBLISHERS**
An imprint of PRENTICE HALL
Upper Saddle River, New Jersey  07458

Dedicated to those gray-haired teachers of mine,
Mrs. Cavert, Miss Lacey, and Mrs. Reese,
who taught me to love the process of learning.

*Randall E. Majors*

In loving celebration of the life of Randall E. Majors.

*Joan Marie Yamasaki*

**Library of Congress Cataloging-in-Publication Data**
Majors, Randall E.
  Is this going to be on the test? : and ten other questions that
can save your college career / by Randall E. Majors. — 3rd ed. /
revision author, Joan Marie Yamasaki.
      p.   cm.
  Includes index
  ISBN 0-13-776741-2 (alk. paper)
    1. College student orientation—United States.  2. Study
skills—United States.  I. Yamasaki, Joan Marie.  II. Title.
LB2343.32.M65    1997
378.1'98—dc21                                          96-37963
                                                        CIP

*Publisher:*  Gay Pauley
*Editor:*  Shari Jo Hehr
*Developmental Editor:*  Katie E. Bradford
*Production Editor:*  Ann Waggoner Aken
*Cover Design and Illustration:*  John Wincek/
    Aerocraft Charter Art Service
*Text Illustration:*  John Wincek/Aerocraft Charter Art Service
*Typesetting:*  Andrea Reider

Printed in the United States of America.

10 9 8 7 6 5 4 3 2

ISBN 0-13-776741-2

Prentice-Hall International (UK) Limited, *London*
Prentice-Hall of Australia Pty. Limited, *Sydney*
Prentice-Hall Canada Inc., *Toronto*
Prentice-Hall Hispanoamericana, S.A., *Mexico*
Prentice-Hall of India Private Limited, *New Delhi*
Prentice-Hall of Japan, Inc., *Tokyo*
Simon & Schuster Asia Pte. Ltd., *Singapore*
Editora Prentice-Hall do Brasil, Ltda., *Rio de Janeiro*

# Contents

# Acknowledgments

Randy Majors, who passed away in late 1995, was the best kind of teacher and the best kind of friend, one who showed the way by example. Randy lived the words he wrote, and in the more than 20 years that we were friends and colleagues, I learned from Randy constantly. "What would Randy do?" was my first thought when I faced a problem. The joke was that while I could think of Randy's response, I just couldn't seem to come to it on my own. This time I hope that I got it right. Randy and I worked together on many projects, and I have tried to make the changes in this edition true to his words and thoughts. Randy was a rare gift. I miss his laughter and his insight more than I can say.

Revising his text was not an easy process and I could not have managed it alone. Several people were important in the completion of this project. I am indebted to my editor, Shari Jo Hehr, for her patience, support, and countless helpful suggestions. Throughout the project, Gay Pauley, Publisher, provided assistance and encouragement for which I am grateful. My thanks to reviewers Kelly Brennan of the University of Alabama, Tuscaloosa, and Arthur Edge of Miracosta Community College for their suggestions. Special thanks to Carole Shaw, Northeast State Technical Community College, for her sensitivity to the needs of returning students and her guidance in making the exercises more inclusive and useful to all students.

My sincere gratitude to Dean Ammonds and Gerry Coffey for their kind help and inspiration in keeping things on track. Finally, I am grateful to Chris Alexander, Jennifer Allen, Mary L. Allen, Gloria Horning, and Jan Carl Park, for their love and encouragement, and to my husband, David, who makes it all worthwhile.

*Joan Marie Yamasaki*
*Revision Author*

# Acknowledgments

In addition to the author, many people contribute to a book, whether through ideas or through activities that have helped clarify the writer's thinking. This book is the result of many people's ideas and contributions as they grew from the design and conduct of GS 1000, the Freshman Colloquium, offered at California State University, Hayward. I acknowledge and thank them for their assistance.

The members of the Steering Committee of GS 1000, the Freshman Colloquium, have been extremely helpful in providing guidance and suggestions as to course philosophy, design, and content. Gail Frey, Dick Monson, Doris Yates, Lynn Elkin, Sue Schaeffer, and Maurice Dance have given me much useful and practical insight into making the course and the book come to life.

Equally helpful have been the many instructors who have taught the course and developed exercises used in this text. Of particular inspiration have been Tim Smith, Joan Yamasaki, CeCe Iandoli, Dennis Frese, Arlene Smith, Gail Auletta, Terry Jones, Judy Sakaki, and Lynn Franks.

The trend across American college campuses to develop and offer the first-year seminar course has produced a wide range of useful resources. I express my appreciation to other writers and course planners who have developed materials that were helpful models for the materials included in this text.

I would like to offer my sincere thanks to the following individuals, who reviewed the book and offered suggestions toward its refinement: Mary Gross of Grossmont College, who suggested I add the chapter on financial planning; Thomas Breed of Sauk Valley Community College; and Kate Leard of Tyler Junior College. The book is improved as a result of their efforts.

Another group deserving recognition for the materials in this text are the students of the past three years in GS 1000 at California State University, Hayward. They have been the testing ground for the chapter contents and exercises. Without their feedback and forebearance, none of the materials used in this text would be as helpful or relevant. I have learned my lessons well from them, and I hope that they are aware of the help they have been in this project.

Finally, I wish to thank the many friends and well-wishers who have faithfully put up with discussions of teaching methods and exercises over the past three years. The content of the text reflects these discussions, and much of the credit for the creativity and practicality of the exercises goes to them. They include Chris DeSantis, Elizabeth Mechling, Rudy Busby, CeCe Iandoli, Joan Yamasaki, Steve Ugbah, and Dale Kobler.

*Randall E. Majors*

# Introduction

Welcome to THE FIRST-YEAR SEMINAR! This book has been written to accompany your participation in an introductory "survival skills" course for first-year students in college. These courses have been introduced at colleges all across the country in order to give new students a practical look at what it will take to succeed in college. Students bring a wealth of experience with them when they enter college, yet not all students are able to make an easy transition from their former routines to the demands of college life.

Whether entering college immediately following high school or returning to school after a period of years, students often feel they are not quite ready for the college experience. Many students enter college without a clear set of goals or reasons for being there. Some students enter school without an adequate background in writing or research skills. Others are quite confused and apprehensive about how college will be different from high school. Almost no students, regardless of age or experience, have had specific training in how to study, manage their time, or explore careers.

Students returning to college after several years may have a clear career focus, but may face special challenges in time and money management. In addition, some students may have to make adjustments to situations that differ from those they encountered in the work world. Others may find it difficult to resume long-ago abandoned study habits when faced with the priorities of family and work.

First-year seminars have been designed to give students exactly the skills that they will need to be successful at college. They provide opportunities for first-year students to meet one another and begin building a personal network of friends, to learn to work with faculty members on a personal, one-on-one basis, and to learn to deal with various administrative functions of a university without being intimidated by its size and impersonality.

There are many challenges in entering this new phase of your life, and this course will try to make that adjustment as easy and as successful as possible. This book is an experiential guide to exploring and learning skills essential to success. It is based on the experience of thousands of college students. Their ideas and suggestions provide the content of the book. If you are an outstanding student, you already have discovered and incorporated into your "student style" many of the ideas and techniques suggested in this book. If that is the case, you will be called upon to share your insights with others. On the other hand, if you feel that your style of studying, learning, and planning could use some improvement, then this textbook is designed to help you discover practical and simple ways of increasing your success skills.

You have taken the first step toward achieving success by enrolling in this course. The skills you will learn here will help you on your way to accomplishing your goals for college success.

## What Is Success?

SUCCESS—that is the name of the game when it comes to college. Your entire college experience will be a contest of mind, heart, and spirit: studying, testing, exploring, playing, experiencing, arguing, writing, talking, thinking, broadening, and growing. Your performance in each of these activities will be challenged and measured, and at the end of your college career, you will answer the question for yourself: was it worth it?

Every student wants to succeed, but not every one does. What is the difference between students who are successful and those who are not? The answer to that question is what this first-year seminar is all about: discovering and using *specific skills for success* in your college career.

One of the problems in being successful, no matter what the endeavor, is knowing how to measure the results. As Alice found in the Looking Glass World, "If you don't know where you are going, any road will take you there."

What does success in college mean to you? Is it high grades or just-passing grades? Is it exploring and discovering new opportunities or sticking to the goals you have already set for yourself? Is it meeting new friends and partying or concentrating on going to class and studying? Perhaps it is a balance of several of these, or you might be coming to college for reasons that are yours alone. All of these are possible goals for success. So you can see there is a problem with defining "success." It will be different for each person.

This course helps solve the problem by focusing on the processes by which people become successful, no matter what their individual goals might be. Amazingly, even though people might have widely different ideas of what constitutes success, the ones who end up satisfied usually have used similar methods for accomplishing their goals. They have used the same processes to ensure their success.

The contents of this course, then, have come from asking students how they became successful. You can also gather this information by observing people yourself. Look around you. What are the successful students doing that makes them able to accomplish so much? No matter what a student's major, grade point average, career aspirations, or life story, success comes by applying the processes of clear thinking, good planning, and attention to detail.

The reliable skills of success in college consist of these processes, which form an outline of this textbook:

- having *clear goals* and knowing what you want from your college experience;
- being able to *manage your time;*
- having the ability to *make good decisions* so that you can solve problems;
- knowing *how to study* efficiently and effectively;
- having the *skills of test-taking* so that exams are an accurate measure of what you know;
- being familiar with the *library and research techniques;*
- knowing *how to write and speak well* to express thoughts clearly and easily;
- having the skills of positive interpersonal *relationships with instructors;*
- knowing where to get *advice and counseling* when necessary;
- doing *financial planning* and personal budget management;
- becoming aware of *cultural differences* and the challenges unique to each different group of students on campus;
- developing *career goals and plans.*

These skills are useful not only for college success. They are the foundation for success throughout your life. Being successful in looking for a job, getting ahead in a career, establishing good interpersonal relationships, finding a sense of satisfaction and fulfillment in your personal life—all of these are based on the processes this course addresses.

Exercise 1 at the end of this introduction is designed to provide you with an overview of the success areas this course will cover. Turn to it and complete Exercise 1 before continuing to read the rest of this introduction.

## Overview of the Course

You now probably have some idea of the scope and content of this book. You have already started evaluating certain parts of the book as being more interesting and valuable to you than others. You may think you already know most of this information. Or perhaps you have never even considered these chapters as topics for study. All of those responses are reasonable. The objective of the exercise was merely to get you to start thinking critically about what you will be studying.

(Parenthetically, this review technique is an excellent method to use in every class you will take in college. A good overview of the structure and content of a textbook and course will help you in planning your study strategy for that class. Are you reading this chapter voluntarily before the first class meeting, or have you waited until your instructor forced you to read it?)

No matter how well they have performed in the past, most students agree that their success skills could be improved. Few students have systematically assessed their own abilities in time management, studying, or getting higher grades. Moreover, almost no students have taken a class that trains them in these skills. This book will benefit you most if you emphasize the areas that best fit your own needs.

Exercise 2 will help you determine the areas in which you already have skills and those to which you may want to give more attention. Knowing how to focus your energies is an important time management tool (as Chapter 1 will cover), so it is good to know where to focus your energy for this class.

By analyzing and discussing Exercise 2, you will develop a clearer idea of the parts of the book that can be most beneficial to you and those areas in which you might be able to help others develop skill. Students learn much from one another, and one of the goals of this course is to introduce you to the concept of peer **mentoring**: sharing your skills and knowledge with other students to help them develop their abilities. If you are a skilled student, you can learn a great deal by trying to train others in those same skills.

Exercise 3 will help you to analyze your strengths and weaknesses in the skill areas this course covers and to consider methods for sharing them with other students.

## How to Use This Book

Every class of the first-year seminar will be slightly different because individual instructors adapt to the unique needs and interests of each individual class. Likewise, instructors have their own unique interests and concerns, which will be reflected in the way they structure and conduct the class. In general, instructors will use this text as a starting place for the course, but you should work closely with your individual instructor to determine the following:

- which of the exercises will be assigned,
- deadlines for completing them,
- special instructions for the exercises, and
- any additional assignments for the course.

This book has been designed to be used interactively. The margins are wide, and key terms are highlighted in bold print. As you read each chapter, make notes in the margins to help you remember the key concepts. You might also write questions to ask your instructor if the material is unclear or if it starts you thinking about a topic on which your instructor might be able to shed more light. You can then use the margin notes you have created to review the most important points in the chapter. At the end of each chapter are exercises designed for you to apply the information you have learned in chapter reading. Do the exercises, even if they are not assigned by your instructor, for deeper understanding of the chapter contents. That way, you can take even greater responsibility for your own learning. The more you interact with the book, the more insight you will gain into the information contained in the chapters.

## Closing Thoughts

Ultimately, people do not learn from books; they learn from their experiences in the world and their interactions with other people. The information provided in this text is only as good as your relationship with your instructor, so talk with him or her about questions or concerns you have as they arise throughout the term. Instructors usually will have many good ideas to add to the suggestions included in this book. If any of the exercises, assignments, or ideas in the book are unclear, ask your instructor for clarification.

No one can be forced to learn. You learn only when you are ready and motivated. If the information in this book does not motivate you, look at your reasons. If the material is too obvious, perhaps you can become a peer mentor for someone who has not yet mastered these skills. When your class discusses the techniques suggested here, you may be able to add others. If the material seems too theoretical, talk about it with friends to see how they use the techniques. They may have found much more practical methods than are included here. Finally, if the material seems too idealistic, remember that the purpose of this book is to talk about SUCCESS, not just minimal survival. If you want your college experience to be of high quality and real significance, it will take high-quality effort. It is idealistic to think that you can excel at every skill included in this book, but you can give each area a full effort. If you combine that effort with the suggestions provided here, your college experience will improve dramatically!

# Reviewing This Textbook

*Instructions: Review the content of this book by investigating the following issues.*

1. Read the Table of Contents for each chapter heading. As you read, consider the following questions and jot down short answers in the form below.

   ■ What are your initial thoughts about what is included in the book? Are you surprised by what is included, or is it what you expected?

   ■ Which chapter looks the most interesting to you? Why?

2. Flip through the pages of this book and notice how the information is presented in the chapters.
   - Approximately how long will it take you to read each chapter?

   - How difficult does the level of language in the text look?

3. Read two or three of the exercises at the end of the chapters.
   - Are the exercises explained clearly?

   - Do they look like they might be interesting to complete?

4. Overall, if the book is a reflection of the entire course, how interesting and valuable do you think the class is going to be? What would make the course more interesting or valuable to you?

# Assessing Your Success Skills

*Instructions: Assess your strengths and weaknesses in the following success skill areas by rating yourself on the following scale.*

(1) very weak   (2) weak   (3) average   (4) strong   (5) very strong

*Goal Setting*

1. How clearly do you understand how college will
   differ from high school or your previous experiences?     1  2  3  4  5
2. How strong is your commitment to be successful at
   college, no matter the effort required?                   1  2  3  4  5

*Time Management*

3. How well do you manage your time
   (e.g., "always running late" versus "on time")?           1  2  3  4  5
4. How effective are your decision-making skills?            1  2  3  4  5

*Study Skills*

5. How effective generally are your present study
   skills (reading, note taking)?                            1  2  3  4  5
6. How usable and complete are your class notes?             1  2  3  4  5

*Test-taking Skills*

7. Generally, how well prepared do you feel to take
   exams and tests?                                          1  2  3  4  5
8. How effectively do you use pre-test aids (e.g.,
   practice questions, study groups, and review sessions)?   1  2  3  4  5
9. How well do you manage test-taking anxiety?               1  2  3  4  5

*Library Research Skills*

10. How efficient are your present library research skills
    (e.g., "time-consuming" versus "able to find
    information quickly")?                                   1  2  3  4  5
11. How familiar are you with the resources in your
    campus library?                                         1  2  3  4  5

*Writing Skills*

12. How effectively can you write an essay or an essay
    answer on an exam?                                       1  2  3  4  5
13. How comfortable do you feel about planning and
    presenting a public speech?                              1  2  3  4  5


*Understanding Instructors*

14. How strong is your ability to get along
    cooperatively with most instructors?                     1  2  3  4  5
15. How often do you seek out instructors
    for help outside class?                                  1  2  3  4  5


*Using Advisers*

16. How effectively do you seek out advice from
    advisers in class selection and planning?                1  2  3  4  5
17. How clearly do you understand the requirements
    for graduation at your school?                           1  2  3  4  5


*Campus Resources*

18. How familiar are you with the way your
    school is organized administratively?                    1  2  3  4  5
19. How familiar are you with services that your
    school provides to students (e.g., health
    center, counseling, learning center)?                    1  2  3  4  5


*Career Planning*

20. How clear are your personal career goals?                1  2  3  4  5
21. How familiar are you with the career-assistance
    services at your school?                                 1  2  3  4  5


TOTAL SCORE at beginning of course: _____

TOTAL SCORE at end of course: _____

# Analyzing Your Success Strengths and Weaknesses

*Instructions: Given your review of the areas covered by this text and your assessment of your own skills in these areas, answer the following questions regarding your strengths and weaknesses.*

1. Of all the skill areas previewed thus far, in which one do you feel most skilled and knowledgeable?

2. Where did you develop this skill?

3. Would you be willing to share this knowledge and skill with another student? If you would like to make a concerted effort to help someone develop his or her skills in this area, how would you design a peer mentoring program to assist this student?

4. From the other skill areas covered in this text, list the five that you think are most important to develop in this class. For each one, discuss briefly what you think you need to do to improve in that area.

- Area 1:



- Area 2:



- Area 3:



- Area 4:



- Area 5:

# 1

---

## "What am I doing here?"

Why have you come to college? People have many different answers for that question. A poll of students revealed the following range of reasons for pursuing a college degree:

- to feel better that I accomplished something;
- to be able to get a respectable job in a career of my choice;
- to get to know my capabilities;
- to gain self-confidence;
- to be a more knowledgeable, well-rounded person;
- so people will look up to me;
- to be able to accept other people's views and ideas;
- to try different fields and select a career that suits me;

- to be a better parent to my children;
- so I will have a better lifestyle;
- to advance in my current job;
- to learn how to deal with the twists and turns that life throws at me;
- education is the only way to better myself;
- no one can take away the education and experience I get here;
- so one of these days I will have my own office and can put my feet up on the desk!

These statements reflect the goals students have for their college education: to accomplish, to get a job, to discover untapped dimensions of personality, to achieve status and wealth. This chapter will explore the issue of goal setting and techniques for using goals to help you be successful.

## Why Are Goals So Important to Success?

Did any of the goals in the list ring true for you? Think about your reasons for attending college for a moment. Exercise 5 at the end of this chapter asks you to list them and to consider the sacrifices you are making to attend college. Stop for a moment and complete Exercise 5 before continuing.

Whatever your reasons for coming to college, it is important to be aware of them, because having clear objectives is one of the best ways to ensure your success. Having a clear set of goals helps you contend with the frustrations and annoyances of daily life. No institution is perfect. Situations will arise in which you get irritated. Instructors might be demanding, unfair, or hard to understand. You occasionally will encounter clerks or administrators who are unhelpful, apathetic, or even downright unfriendly to you. (Fortunately, they are the rare exception rather than the rule.) People without clear goals often just "throw in the towel" in response to these situations. For them, college is not worth the hassle. On the other hand, students with clear goals have the motivation to confront the problem and find ways to overcome it.

Where do goals come from? People develop goals in the same way they develop personality—both from inner drives and from the environment in which they are nurtured. Thus, people from the same background may develop different goals because of their differing inner natures. Likewise, people from dissimilar environments may share the same goals because of the kind of people they are on the inside. In terms of success, the source of a goal is not nearly as important as its strength. If a person believes in a goal strongly enough, almost nothing in the world will be able to stop her from achieving it.

If you are fortunate, you grew up in an environment that encouraged you to set high goals and gave you the confidence that you could achieve them. Some fortunate students even have **support systems,** people behind them who provide emotional support (such as encouragement and pride in their accomplishments), physical support (such as financial assistance or transportation or housing), and training support (such as a good educational foundation in the skills needed to be a success). People who have these resources usually have clear, positive goals and are confident in their abilities to achieve them.

Even without this background, however, individuals with strong inner drive can have firm goals and be confident about success. Life is sometimes harder for them because they do not have the environmental support that comes from good support systems, but it is possible to be just as successful. These individuals need to work hard to build their own support systems in the new situation into which they have arrived. Finding supportive friends, avoiding situations or people who tempt you to give up, and learning skills for coping with the frustration and anxiety of hardships will reinforce your achievement of goals.

## How Will College Differ from Past Experiences?

College offers a new world of experiences and opportunities for students. One of the biggest sources of frustration for new freshmen is figuring out the adjustment from high school norms and expectations to those of college. Things are not the same; they are worlds apart! Those who decide to return to college after being away from an educational setting for several years may find themselves having to adjust to new methods and new systems. Some students may have entered college to advance their careers or to make a career change. Others may have decided to return to school after raising children, serving in the military, or retiring. Success in college may require different skills than these students needed to do well in their previous positions. In addition to learning new ways of doing things, returning students often are faced with balancing the needs of their families and jobs in addition to the demands of college. To be successful in this new setting, students must carefully analyze their old ways of doing things and discover new skills that will help them survive and be successful. Exercise 4 asks you to start thinking about how college will differ from high school or your previous experiences. Complete it now.

The major difference between high school and college lies in the issue of *personal responsibility.* In college no one is going to select your major or your courses for you. Instructors often do not notice whether you come to class or not. There are no study halls to force you to prepare for class. No one monitors your coursework and warns you that you might be failing a class. All of these functions you must learn to do on your own. Unfortunately, some students do not have the self-control to make sure these activities get done, so they end up suffering the consequences.

College demands a whole new attitude toward responsibility. You must become responsible for your own success because the system is not set up to watch out for you. The university makes some attempts to be helpful—advisers are assigned, counselors are available—but, by and large, students are left to fend for themselves when selecting courses, getting grades, and making decisions in personal life issues.

The solution to this situation is to become more responsible—to get control of your time, to make strong commitments to attending class, to seek out and take advantage of the help that is available, and to find the secret techniques of success that will make your life easier. This course will attempt to introduce you to some of these secrets of success, but it is up to you to incorporate them into your student style.

A second major difference between high school (no matter how long ago you attended) and college is in the *investment factor.* A college degree entails a huge investment of your time and resources. Even if you are not paying an exorbitant tuition, you are sacrificing the money you could have made if you were working. You are also putting in a great amount of time and hard work. What is the payoff? Most students realize that college will improve their earning income potentials in later careers (on the average, from $500,000 to $1 million). If you calculate the relationship between the number of days you will spend in college and your improved income, you will see that each day of college training is worth from $1,000 to $2,000 or more to you. Another benefit is that personal satisfaction levels in careers and lifestyle are much higher for college graduates.

Given these possible rewards, however, some students do not see college as an opportunity for personal growth. Rather, they see it as they saw high school—something that had to be endured to get into the "real world." These two opposite attitudes create the low-motivation profile or the high-motivation profile in students.

Do you know students with the low-motivation profile? Chances are great that they will not do well in college, nor will they get the maximum benefits that a college education can provide. In contrast is the profile of a different kind of student, one who will be much more likely to achieve at a high level and enjoy the process of education.

Success in college demands a high-motivation profile. Without this internal motivation, chances of a student staying in school are much lower, and, even if the student does stay, it will not be a very enjoyable experience.

So which is it with you? Being honest with yourself, which profile do you fit? If you do have elements of the low-motivation type, do you want to change them?

---

*The Low-Motivation Profile*

See college as just something to do until something better comes along.

Make time for class and study by squeezing them in among more important activities such as work or socializing.

Want to do the minimum work possible to get a grade.

Look for the easiest way out when selecting courses.

See instructors and the college system as set on making life miserable.

---

---

*The High-Motivation Profile*

See college as an opportunity to develop themselves in ways that will help them meet their long-term life goals.

Commit the time necessary for attending class and studying to produce high-quality work.

Look for ways to make classes more valuable by going beyond just the minimum.

Select classes that will challenge them and develop their potential.

Look at the college experience with tolerance and patience for its shortcomings, but with determination to take advantage of its possibilities.

---

# Techniques for Successful Goal Setting

If your goals for being in college are not clear, or if you want to create more internal motivation with your goals, the following suggestions will be helpful. Goal setting is a highly individual task, but it is useful to discuss your ideas with people whose opinions you trust. It takes a long time to clarify some life goals, and they may change over time so be patient with yourself. In order to change and grow personally, you have to be more tolerant of ambiguity and new experiences.

The following techniques will be useful for clarifying your goals.

1. **Look at goals in various aspects of your life.** All aspects of your life are guided by the goals you have. In college, you will probably have goals in many areas: intellectual, social, emotional, recreational, and occupational. Exercise 6 at the end of this chapter asks you to think about and clarify your goals in these areas.

2. **Be specific about your goals.** Whenever possible, set goals in terms you can measure and with time frames you can try to keep. These specifics will help you see how well you are doing on the way to accomplishing the goals you have set.

3. **Be positive in setting your goals.** It is more effective to try to accomplish a positive action than to avoid a negative one. When you set goals, use positive language that states what you want and do not use negative language about what you do not want or what you are trying to avoid.

4. **Be realistic in setting your goals.** It is fine to set high goals for yourself, but you should always measure these against the realistic limitations of the situation. Goals that are impossibly high only serve to discourage and defeat the person who sets them.

5. **Gather information to clarify your goals.** If you are vague or uninformed about possible goals, explore and investigate to get the information you need to make a decision. Talk with knowledgeable and experienced people about your goals. The more you know, the easier it is to set good goals.

6. **Be willing to change or adjust goals if necessary.** As you get new information or experience, you may occasionally have to reevaluate and set new goals. In a changing world, you have to change or be left behind, but change only when you have good reasons to do so.

7. **Be objective about obstacles that arise.** Every goal is going to be met with barriers that must be overcome. Your task is to discover all the available means for overcoming the obstacles you face. This is what makes life challenging and success so sweet. If confronted with impossibly difficult obstacles, however, you need to assess how realistic your goals are and develop an alternative plan of action.

8. **Talk about your goals as you make decisions.** Every time you are faced with a decision, question how your action will affect your long-term goals. You can coordinate your efforts, which will help you achieve your goals, or you can fritter away your energy in many different directions, which will only hinder accomplishing your goals. A clear vision of your long-term objectives will help you make good short-term decisions.

9. **Listen to other people's goals.** Everyone needs someone to talk to, and listening is one of the best ways to learn about the goals, obstacles, and solutions that other people have found in their life's path. By listening and sharing with others, you will learn much about yourself. You can help them, and they can help you to clarify, strategize, and empathize.

10. **Make goal setting a high priority as a freshman.** It is easy to let the task of setting goals slip by when you are a freshman. There are so many interesting things to do! You should be

careful of the **activity trap,** however, in becoming so involved in the short-term hustle and bustle that you overlook the need for long-term planning. The clearer your goals are as you begin your college education, the more likely you will be to make them come true.

## Closing Thoughts

One final thought should be said about college expectations and goal setting. People generally find in college what they expect to find. Those who expect it to be a pain in the neck tend to find that to be the case. Those who expect college to be a liberating and an exciting growth opportunity are usually not disappointed. Ultimately, you get out of college what you put into it.

Will a college degree be just a piece of paper to you, or will it be a life-changing and enriching experience? The choice is up to you.

## Observing How College Differs from High School or Previous Experiences

Complete Part A if you have been out of high school for fewer than two years, and complete Part B if you have been out of high school for more than two years.

**Part A**

*Instructions: Based on what you have experienced of college thus far and on what you expect in the future, list the ways (as many as you can think of) in which college will differ from your high school experience in the following categories.*

|  | HIGH SCHOOL | COLLEGE |
| --- | --- | --- |
| Type of fellow students |  |  |
| Type of classes (size, difficulty, subjects) |  |  |
| Type of instructors |  |  |

|                              | HIGH SCHOOL | COLLEGE |
| ---------------------------- | ----------- | ------- |
| Extracurricular activities   |             |         |
| Employment while in school   |             |         |
| Time demands                 |             |         |
| Personal growth opportunities |            |         |

**Part B**

*Instructions: Based on what you have experienced of college thus far and on what you expect in the future, list the ways in which college will differ from your previous experience in the following categories.*

|  | PREVIOUS EXPERIENCE | COLLEGE |
| --- | --- | --- |
| Scheduling of time |  |  |
| Diversity of people |  |  |
| Degree of authority |  |  |
| Type of environment |  |  |

| | PREVIOUS EXPERIENCE | COLLEGE |
|---|---|---|
| Employment | | |
| Family/Community responsibilities | | |
| Personal growth opportunities | | |

# Determining Your Reasons for Attending College

*Instructions: Answer the following questions to determine your personal goals and motivation level for attending college.*

1. What are you personal reasons for attending college? List as many as you can think of.

2. What sacrifices are you aware of making to attend school?

3. How does attendance at college fit into your life plan?

# Setting Your Personal Goals

*Instructions:*

*Step 1. In the following five areas of growth, list goals you have for your college career. Also consider how your college experiences may contribute to your growth in your current work and family situation.*

- **Intellectual Growth.** What subjects do you want to study? What courses in the college catalogue look interesting to you? What are some things you want to learn that you have never experienced before?

- **Social Growth.** What kinds of people do you want to meet? Who do you anticipate will be your friends? What organizations would you like to become involved in?

- **Emotional Growth.** Which aspects of your personality would you like to develop or get more under control? If you expect stress levels to be higher, what do you plan to do to manage them?

- **Recreational Growth.** What physical activities do you want to pursue while in school? How do you want to develop physically. What activities will help you do that?

- **Professional Growth.** Which career areas would you like to know more about? Do you have a chosen career path already? How much do you know about that goal?

*Step 2. Now that you have set some goals, go back and critique them with a partner in terms of the techniques for successful goal setting discussed in this chapter.*

- Can you measure the results?
- Are they specific in terms of time?
- Are they stated in positive language?
- Are they realistic?

*Rewrite any goal statements that do not meet these criteria.*

# Determining Your Success Assets and Liabilities

*Instructions:* *Most people have both advantages and disadvantages when it comes to college success. Explore your assets (support systems) and your liabilities (obstacles you have to overcome) by answering the following questions.*

1. What kinds of support systems are behind you to help you succeed in school?

   ▪ **Emotional support** (people who want you to succeed and are encouraging you)

   ▪ **Physical support** (financial aid and actual help with things such as housing, transportation, food, clothing, books, tuition)

   ▪ **Training support** (people who have worked with you in the past or who will be available in the future to provide you with the skills and motivation to succeed)

2. What is the biggest obstacle you see that you will have to overcome to be successful in college?

3. What are some of the ways in which you think you can begin to overcome the obstacle you mention above? (Share the problem with someone whose opinion you trust and see if he or she has any ideas.)

4. What person(s) from your past would you particularly like to thank for having prepared you to be successful in college? What did these people do to help you? You might consider writing them a note to express your thanks.

# 2

# "How am I going to get everything done?"

A wise person once said, "Time is precious—because there is always so little of it." Is time a precious resource that you have trouble managing? Do you find yourself constantly running up against the problem of too much to do and not enough time to do it?

Most people admit they are not very good managers of time. Critical indicators of time management problems include the following:

- consistently being late for meetings or deadlines;
- always feeling pressured and under the gun;
- never having enough time to get everything done;
- making errors because of time pressure;

- forgetting important dates and events;
- never having time to relax and enjoy life.

Unfortunately, if time management has been a problem for you in the past, things are only going to get worse as you move to college. You will spend less time in class meetings, but you will probably have much more studying and greater research responsibilities for each class. The final exam crunch of papers, assignments, and tests at the end of the term may be much greater than you ever experienced before. You may also have to spend more time at a job than you did in high school. And, hopefully, your social life will demand more of your time as you meet new friends at school. Thus, time management can be a vital skill to help you balance and find the time for all these things you want to do.

Effective time management requires a commitment. There are no easy and simple solutions to the problems of busy and demanding schedules. Hard choices and determination are the only way to make time work for you rather than against you. But if you do want to be in control of your time instead of it being in control of you, four tools can be of help: a schedule, a calendar, a "To Do" list, and a model for making good decisions. This chapter introduces you to these four techniques and discusses methods for using them effectively.

## Make a Schedule to Organize Your Week

A **weekly schedule** can help you organize your time in each seven-day period. Most people have regularly repeating weekly schedules, and a printed outline of that schedule will show you at a glance how your time should be assigned through the week.

Exercise 8 at the end of this chapter asks you to complete a weekly schedule for your own use. When planning your weekly schedule, use the following guidelines.

1. First enter your regular **sleeping hours.** Plan to give yourself enough time to get adequate rest. This should be one of your first priorities, because quality work in other areas depends on your getting enough rest at night. If you have to rise early, plan on getting to bed earlier than usual the night before. Likewise, if you "sleep in" on weekends, put that into your schedule.

2. Next enter your regular **eating hours.** Regular meals are an important source of strength to maintain your stamina and concentration. If you skip meals, consider taking the time to change that habit and include them in your schedule. Mealtimes can serve double duty both as rest periods in a busy schedule and as times to spend with family or socialize with friends.

3. Now you are ready to add your **work hours** if you are employed. If these change from week to week, you have to learn to be flexible with the other elements of your schedule to make sure everything else gets included.

4. Next enter your **school classes.** These usually meet regularly, so they will be easy to remember. Make sure to add special events and field trips, however, if they occur in unusual weeks.

5. Include the **study periods** you will need to do homework, read, and do research. Each class will differ as to the number of hours outside class you will need, so learn to analyze each class as it begins so you can accurately calculate the number of study hours you will need.

6. Now enter the time you need for **family/friends and community activities.** Add the time that you need to take your children to school, to accompany your parents to regular medical appointments, or catch up with your friend about her new job.

7. Enter your regular **exercise and activity periods.** Most people find that regularly scheduling exercise is the only way they find time to do it. Likewise, if you have regularly scheduled meetings with clubs or groups, they should be included in your schedule.

8. Include **free time and rest periods** in your schedule. If you watch TV during free time, select the programs you want to watch and include them. Many people scan the TV guide when it first comes out each week and note special programs they want to be sure to watch. Everyone needs free time to relax and rest. Remember to include this in your schedule.

The chart on the next page illustrates what a typical college student's schedule might look like. Notice how it includes all the elements discussed above: sleep, eating, work, class, study, exercise, and free time.

Making a weekly schedule is not enough. You also must know how to use it effectively in managing your time. The following suggestions will help you use a schedule to your best advantage.

1. **Be realistic.** It does not do any good to have an elaborate, carefully drawn schedule if you are not going to stick to it or if it does not reflect the way you really spend your time. The point of having a schedule is to help you learn to control your time. If you insist on being out of control, the problems of time management will never be solved.

2. **Let your schedule evolve naturally.** Observe yourself for a week or two before you plan your schedule. How do you actually spend your time? Let your schedule grow out of the way you really do spend your time, then gradually try to bring the unproductive or wasted time periods under control.

# Sample Weekly Student Schedule

|      | Sun | Mon | Tue | Wed | Thur | Fri | Sat |
|------|-----|-----|-----|-----|------|-----|-----|
| 6    |     |     |     |     |      |     |     |
| 7    | Breakfast |  |     |     |      |     |  →  |
| 8    | Catch up! | English | Errands | English | Work | English | Work |
| 9    |     |     |     |     |      |     |     |
| 10   | Work | History | Fresh. Seminar | History |  | History |  |
| 11   |     |     |     |     |      |     |     |
| 12   |     | Lunch |   |     |   →  |     |     |
| 1    |     |     | Library time |  |  | Study |  |
| 2    |     | Study |     | Physics lab |  |     |     |
| 3    |     |     |     |     |      |     |     |
| 4    |     |     | Physics |  | Physics |  |  |
| 5    |     | Exercise |  | Exercise |  | Exercise |  |
| 6    | ←   | Dinner |   |     |      |     |  →  |
| 7    | Study |   | Shop for groceries |  | Work | Free time/ family | Free time/ family |
| 8    |     | Study |     | Study |     |     |     |
| 9    |     |     |     |     |      |     |     |
| 10   |     |     |     |     |      |     |     |
| 11   |     |     |     |     |      |     |     |

3. **Try to change only a little at a time.** Learning effective time management is like losing weight: you cannot do it all overnight. It is best to change only one or two things in a schedule and get them under control before you move on to other things. So for your first schedule you might want to include only a few of the ideas suggested here. If those work well, you can move on to other elements later.

4. **Avoid overscheduling yourself.** Some people think that every minute of the day has to be accounted for, so they plan activities for every waking moment and forget that they need time to get from one place to another and that things sometimes take longer than anticipated. Thus, their entire schedules get thrown off because they have been unrealistic about the amount they can actually accomplish. You have to have a realistic idea of how much you can do in one week and then learn to cut back if you are trying to do too much. Remember also that the best laid plans often go awry, so give yourself some slack to compensate for times when things do not go as planned.

When planning or selecting classes, keep an eye toward how they will affect your schedule. Include study periods between classes as you select your class schedule. If you cram all the classes together without any breaks between them, you are more likely to want to "blow off" the rest of the afternoon once you are out of that big block of classes. Breaks for meals, exercise, and study should be scattered among classes and work sessions.

## Use a Calendar

While the weekly schedule helps you get your week under control, keeping a calendar can help you in long-term planning over months. The calendar is for recording and remembering special events such as exams, term projects, one-of-a-kind assignments, conferences, and meetings that happen only occasionally. On the social side, keeping a calendar will help you plan for and remember special events such as birthdays, anniversaries, parties, and social obligations.

Exercise 9 provides you with a three-month calendar to use during this current school term. Following are some suggestions to assist you in using your calendar.

1. **Find a calendar form you like.** You may not find the calendar pages in Exercise 9 convenient. Find a calendar you do like, such as a pocket version or one that fits inside your notebook.

2. **Keep your calendar with you at all times.** Always have your calendar handy when you are at work and school, because those are the two times when special events are most likely to happen. At home, keep your calendar close to your phone to record appointments and social events.

3. **Record events on your calendar as soon as they arise.** The first period of each class is usually spent on planning the term's events. As soon as you know when exams, speeches, assignments, and reports are due, enter them on your calendar.

4. **Enter meetings and conferences as soon as you make the date.** If you rely on your memory, you will invariably forget one.

5. **Avoid end-of-term time crunch by staggering the due dates.** Instructors are often willing to be lenient about deadlines if you plan in advance. If you cannot delay a deadline, you could always get the work done earlier than necessary.

6. **Build in checkpoints for long-term projects.** For large assignments, break the work into smaller units and give yourself some intermediate due dates for the various parts of the project. In this way, you will avoid huge amounts of work due at the last minute.

## Use "To Do" Lists

The "To Do" list is a listing of things you want to accomplish on a certain day or within the week. Just like a shopping list that helps you remember what to pick up in the supermarket, the To Do list reminds you of what you need to get accomplished within the day.

To Do lists are also useful for **prioritizing** activities by rank-ordering the most important ones so you get those done first. If things farther down on the list do not get done, you can always carry them over to the next day.

You can use weekly To Do lists for all the things you want to accomplish in a given week. Many people use them as daily lists for each day's activities as well. It is best to have a regular planning session, either on Sunday night or early on Monday morning to lay out the activities you want to accomplish during the week. For the daily To Do list, the night before or the first thing in the morning is the best for planning.

When writing the To Do list, it is useful to divide activities into the following three categories:

A = things that absolutely have to get done,

B = things that are important to get done,

C = things that it would be nice to get done but which are not essential and can be carried over until later if necessary.

You might also include estimates of how long you think each item on your list will take. This technique may help you determine how much is realistically possible in any one day.

When using a To Do list for studying purposes, many students set time limits for each activity and then move on to the next to make sure they get all their "A" priorities covered. You should experiment with these various techniques and find the one that works best for you. Exercise 10 gives you an opportunity to try this strategy for managing your time.

The following illustrates one student's To Do list techniques. Note how the first list is just a jot list of things to be accomplished for the day. The second list has prioritized these same items.

| *Jot Item To Do List* | *Prioritized To Do List* |
| --- | --- |
| work on English paper | A: study for |
| take car to shop |    history exam |
| exercise |    exercise |
| call Sam |    meet with adviser |
| start research for project | B: take car to shop |
| study for history exam |    call Sam |
| meet with adviser |    work on English |
| go to the grocery store |    paper |
| | C: start research |
| |    for project |
| |    go to the |
| |    grocery store |

## Follow a Critical Thinking Model to Make Good Decisions

Can you think of a time when you made a poor decision? Why do you think you made a wrong decision? Bad decision makers tend to jump at the first idea that comes to them, and they do not think critically about the quality of the idea or the solution. Careful decision makers determine better choices by carefully generating, testing, implementing, and monitoring their decisions. You can learn to be a good decision maker through the use of a critical thinking model. Mastering the ability to apply it to various life situations is a worthy goal—one that will involve practice on a continuing basis.

Begin to explore the skill of making good decisions by applying this model to a problem. For example, scheduling your time may present a challenge. As you plan your schedule, you may find that it provides you with the perfect guide for structuring your time. But there is another possibility: the schedule may not work out at all. You may find that you have overstructured your time, underestimated the time needed for commuting or research, or failed to consider urgent circumstances such as overtime at work. You will need to change your schedule. How will you decide about which changes to make so that you can best use your time?

The critical thinking model consists of six steps that enable you to analyze the problem thoroughly and consider possible alternatives. Remember that the more actively involved you are in each step of the process, the better control you have of your options and the final choice. Here are the six steps:

1. **Analyze the situation.** What is the status quo? Why do you need to change things? What will happen if you do nothing? What is the source or cause of the problem situation? What outcome do you want for this situation?

2. **Identify alternative solutions.** What possible responses would change the situation? What have other people done in similar situations? What would not work in this situation? Who can help you identify more options?

3. **Evaluate the alternatives.** What solution did you try in the past? Why did it fail? How will each of the alternatives affect the situation? What is the cost or downside of each alternative? What are the consequences of each choice? Does a possible solution create more problems than it is worth?

4. **Select the best course of action.** Which is the most effective solution with the least downside? Are there back-up alternatives in case the "best" one does not work?

5. **Implement the best solution.** How can you best implement the decision? Do you need someone's assistance to do so? What resources do you need to implement it? How much time will it take?

6. **Monitor the decision.** Are you fairly certain the decision will create the desired outcome? Are there any unforeseen side effects that are problematic? Does the solution actually solve the problem situation? If not, which of the remaining alternatives will you implement next?

You can apply the steps of the critical thinking model not only to scheduling your time but to every decision that you must make. When you use the critical thinking model effectively, you are constantly employing the principles of feedback and course correction. Seek feedback from knowledgeable people at every step of the process because you may not recognize or be aware of all aspects of the situation, possible alternatives, or potential downsides. As you identify and evaluate alternatives, you need the feedback of other people who are observing or have experience with the process. Their insight can help you analyze and evaluate your options so that you make the best decision. Feedback is vital in the monitoring process to make sure that the decision you make actually produces the outcome you want. If it does not, or if it produces undesirable side effects, you may need to go back to the initial steps of the critical thinking model and find a better solution. Exercise 11 asks you to apply this model to a poor decision you have made in the past.

# Closing Thoughts

Time management should be an aid in organizing your day, not just one more task to feel guilty about or to cause you stress. Do not become compulsive about organizing your time. Find a system that works well for you, and watch whether your time is under control. If you need more control of your time, follow the techniques suggested in this chapter. When exploring the methods that work best for you, keep the following tips in mind.

1. **Take it easy on yourself.** Time management is difficult for most people, and you do not want to overburden yourself by trying to do too much. If you have too much to do for the time you have available, no amount of time management will help you get it all done.

2. **Give yourself plenty of time for sleep, rest, and relaxation.** These activities are often overlooked in a busy schedule, but they are vital if you are going to remain alert and healthy. They reduce stress and help you perform your other tasks at a high level. Be sure to include them in your schedule.

3. **Avoid procrastination.** When you have to get things done, it is better to start now rather than later. Things only get more difficult when you put them off, because you add the pressure of working under the gun. If you want to enjoy your college classes and activities, you have to give them plenty of time to grow and develop naturally. Always being on the run and late for things will not help make them more enjoyable.

4. **Leave room for emergencies.** Extraordinary things will always happen: car breakdowns, sudden illnesses, the dog eating your homework, or whatever. Leave time in your schedule to compensate for these unexpected events. If you have scheduled every available minute, there is no flexibility to adapt to the unexpected.

5. **Remember your commitment.** All these techniques sound rather overwhelming if time management is new to you. But by trying them just a little at a time and then adding new techniques as you become more successful, you can master your time.

Your need to make good, practical, ethical decisions will continue throughout your lifetime. Long after your graduation, you will be faced with situations that demand thorough and careful assessment. The critical thinking model provides you with a system for evaluating options, anticipating consequences, and making appropriate choices. Many exercises in this text require you to make decisions. As you complete these exercises, try to apply the critical thinking model to develop skill in using this model. Also, try using this model next time you face a decision in your life outside the classroom. See if it helps you to explore all of the possibilities before you make a decision.

# Planning Your Master Schedule

*Instructions: In the form on the following page, plan your weekly master schedule for the coming term. Check off each of the following activities as you place it into your schedule. On this page, write any notes to yourself about ways in which you can manage your time more effectively for each of these activities.*

☐ Sleep:

☐ Classes:

☐ Family/Friends:

☐ Exercise/Recreation:

☐ Eating:

☐ Study:

☐ Community Activities:

☐ Free Time:

☐ Work:

|     | Sun | Mon | Tue | Wed | Thur | Fri | Sat |
| --- | --- | --- | --- | --- | --- | --- | --- |
| 6 |  |  |  |  |  |  |  |
| 7 |  |  |  |  |  |  |  |
| 8 |  |  |  |  |  |  |  |
| 9 |  |  |  |  |  |  |  |
| 10 |  |  |  |  |  |  |  |
| 11 |  |  |  |  |  |  |  |
| 12 |  |  |  |  |  |  |  |
| 1 |  |  |  |  |  |  |  |
| 2 |  |  |  |  |  |  |  |
| 3 |  |  |  |  |  |  |  |
| 4 |  |  |  |  |  |  |  |
| 5 |  |  |  |  |  |  |  |
| 6 |  |  |  |  |  |  |  |
| 7 |  |  |  |  |  |  |  |
| 8 |  |  |  |  |  |  |  |
| 9 |  |  |  |  |  |  |  |
| 10 |  |  |  |  |  |  |  |
| 11 |  |  |  |  |  |  |  |

# Planning Your Calendar

*Instructions:* *For each of the next three months, write in the calendar the major events that you will want to remember. If you have never used a calendar before, this exercise will help you to discover the worth of recording important dates in managing your time more effectively. Include the following categories of events in your calendar:*

- Homework assignments
- Class projects due
- Meetings
- Family/friends and community activities

- Exams
- Social events
- Key dates to remember
- Work schedule

MONTH _____

| Sun | Mon | Tue | Wed | Thur | Fri | Sat |
|-----|-----|-----|-----|------|-----|-----|
|     |     |     |     |      |     |     |
|     |     |     |     |      |     |     |
|     |     |     |     |      |     |     |
|     |     |     |     |      |     |     |
|     |     |     |     |      |     |     |

MONTH _____

| Sun | Mon | Tue | Wed | Thur | Fri | Sat |
|-----|-----|-----|-----|------|-----|-----|
|     |     |     |     |      |     |     |
|     |     |     |     |      |     |     |
|     |     |     |     |      |     |     |
|     |     |     |     |      |     |     |
|     |     |     |     |      |     |     |

MONTH _____

| Sun | Mon | Tue | Wed | Thur | Fri | Sat |
|-----|-----|-----|-----|------|-----|-----|
|     |     |     |     |      |     |     |
|     |     |     |     |      |     |     |
|     |     |     |     |      |     |     |
|     |     |     |     |      |     |     |
|     |     |     |     |      |     |     |

# Using a Weekly "To Do" List

*Instructions:* *Complete this exercise on a Sunday night or a Monday morning. To familiarize yourself with how a "To Do" list works, complete the following list with the activities you want to accomplish in the coming week. Prioritize them into "A" (must do), "B" (should do), and "C" (like to do). Review your list at the end of each day to see how you are progressing on your list.*

Week of:

- "A" List:

- "B" List:

- "C" List:

Record here your reaction to working with a To Do list. Was it new for you, or have you used this technique before? Was it useful? Did it help you prioritize your time? Did you have many items left over and not done from your original list? What is your general opinion about using a To Do list?

# Using the Critical Thinking Model

*Instructions: Consider a poor decision that you have made. For example, it may have been a decision about the scheduling of your time, the decision to make a purchase, or the decision to behave in a particular way in a relationship. Analyze this decision by going through each of the six steps of the Critical Thinking Model and answering the questions for each step. You might want to do this with a partner who can serve as a "devil's advocate" to help you be more objective. Once you have analyzed the problem with this model, you should have a clearer understanding of why the decision was a poor one and what you could have done to make a more effective decision.*

Poor Decision:

1. **Analyze the situation.**

2. **Identify alternative solutions.**

3. **Evaluate the alternatives.**

4. Select the best course of action.

5. Implement the best solution.

6. Monitor the decision.

# 3

---

## "What do I have to do to get an 'A'?"

Most students never realize that studying is a specific skill in its own right. Few people have ever had a class in or read a book about how to study. Consequently, many people's study skills are the result of trial-and-error learning of study methods. Worse yet, some students have poor study skills that prevent them from reaching their potential and learning effectively. Even though they study diligently, they do not learn thoroughly because of distractions, lack of organizations, or last-minute attempts to cram too much information at once.

You can improve your learning ability, and your grades can improve dramatically, if you systematically analyze the methods you use in studying and learning. This chapter analyzes general study methods proven to be effective and concentrates specifically on how to read a textbook and how to take lecture notes. Later chapters will explore additional ways to improve grades, but this chapter begins with the basics: your own ability to organize and understand the information your instructors present to you in texts and lectures. If you can master these topics first, the other methods for getting higher grades—test-taking skills, research and writing skills, and negotiating with instructors—will be much easier.

## General Study Methods

Long before you sit down with a textbook and try to learn the information in it, you have made decisions that will affect how successful you will be in studying. No matter what the information is, your interests and experience will shape how effectively you master the new information. In order of priority, the factors that affect your ability to learn are listed below.

- The more interested you are in the information, the easier it will be to pay attention and remember.
- The higher your aptitude for the topic, the easier it will be to master the information.
- The more similar the topic is to other things you have mastered, the easier it will be to learn.
- The better your memory skills are developed, the easier it will be to remember the new information.
- The more systematic your approach to the information, the more successful you will be.

The more of these elements you have working in your favor, the easier and better your learning will be. Thus, if you are highly interested in a subject and already skilled in it to some extent, it will be easier to study. Most college subjects, however, will be unfamiliar, so what can you do to make them more interesting? The answer is to select classes that have some potential for being interesting and to work actively to find interest factors in the classes you have to take. Even if a class is uninteresting and unfamiliar, you can use the other elements—improving your memory, and using systematic study skills—to become successful.

So how good are your study skills? Exercise 12 at the end of this chapter asks you to review them. Stop and complete this exercise before continuing the chapter.

The system of study techniques begins with the following general guidelines. Because the techniques have many variations, experiment and find the ones that work most effectively for you. The principle here is to find something that works. Merely falling back on old habits and hoping for the best is the worst approach you can take.

1. **Do research on your classes before they begin.** To determine or to create potential interest in your classes, gather information about them before you actually sign up. Talk to students who have taken the class or visit with the instructor about the scope of the course, the purpose in its being required, and the kinds of reading and assignments required. This information will help you select more interesting courses and understand requirements placed on you.

2. **Begin studying before your classes begin.** Even before the first class session, preview the textbook and read the introduction and opening chapter. This early preview will help you see the scope of the course and understand how it is structured. You will appreciate the first class session much more, and you can more intelligently plan your study strategy for the class.

3. **Study the course syllabus closely.** Good instructors will provide you with a course outline and clear explanations of the assignments required for the class. Study these closely and ask questions about anything you do not understand. Plan your time based on the guidelines your instructors give you. If they do not provide these guidelines, politely suggest how helpful it would be if the instructor would provide them.

4. **Determine your study time needs.** Based on your critique of the syllabuses from each class, plan your time needs. Note where several assignments will come due on the same day or week. Plan your studying so you will not be pressed for time at the end of the term. You may even need to do work earlier than required to give yourself more time at the end.

5. **Study hardest the first two weeks of class.** By rigorously applying yourself the first two weeks of class, you will lay a solid foundation for mastering the material that comes later in the course. The remaining material will be easier to understand and you will not have to work as hard. If you wait until the last two weeks to really apply yourself (as many students do), you will not have adequate time to internalize and learn the material and do the best work possible on class projects.

6. **Have a regular place and time to study.** If at all possible, schedule regular study periods throughout the week and stick to your schedule. Studying consistently at the same place is also a useful technique for some students. To make your studying efficient, find a place with good lighting and no distractions.

7. **Study during the day, not just at night.** Plan study periods during the day when you are fresh and can give close attention to the material. Studying when you are tired or sleepy is not effective for memory or comprehension.

8. **Study in frequent shorter sessions, not in long cram periods.** You retain more information when you break it into smaller units. Study small units of information in short time

blocks—even 15 minutes—during the day. These short blocks are especially effective for review and self-quizzing sessions.

9. **Experiment with a variety of study techniques.** Depending on the nature of your classes, try different ways of studying: tape recording lectures and listening to them in the car as you commute, making flash cards for vocabulary and key concepts, studying old exams for a course, using study guides that provide sample test questions and chapter outlines, and finding a regular **study buddy.** A study buddy is a regular study partner (or several) from the same class who can help you study be reviewing your notes and asking practice questions about key concepts when preparing for exams.

## How to Read a Textbook

There are two basic types of reading: passive and active. **Passive reading** is what you do for leisure. The information is interesting for the moment, but you make no effort to critique or memorize it. **Active reading,** on the other hand, includes higher-order thinking processes such as organizing, critiquing, and memorizing to make sure you understand and integrate the information.

Most textbook reading for college classes demands active reading, but many students are not aware of the difference in these two approaches to a book. The following techniques will help you become an active reader and more successfully integrate the information contained in course textbooks.

1. **Know how important the text is for your class.** Textbooks serve many different functions. In some classes, texts contain the entire content of the course. In others, they are supplemental to the information presented in lectures. You need to know how much you will be tested over the content of a text so you will know how much time to spend studying it. Politely ask your instructors about the weight they will place on the reading. They can give you helpful suggestions about what to study closely and what to breeze through lightly.

2. **Set reading goals.** Divide your reading assignments into manageable units and only try to read a given amount in any one sitting. Plan to do some reading every day, and regularly review the reading you have done in the past week. Do not let the reading pile up until the end of the term; you will not be able to absorb it adequately if you do.

3. **Structure your reading time.** Begin a reading session by previewing what you will read in a single setting. While you are reading, rest occasionally and review what you have read so far. Once you are done reading, review the material at least twice in the following 24 hours to embed it in your memory.

4. **Approach a textbook systematically.** The chart at the end of this section illustrates the SQ3R method for studying. When you approach a new book, read the table of contents first to understand the big picture before you start reading the chapters. Read the introduction or preface to understand the writer's frame of reference. When reading a chapter, first read the introduction, chapter headings, and summary. As you read chapters, stop periodically to review what you have read so far and to see how much is left to cover. Once you have read an entire chapter, review the main points.

5. **Ask yourself questions as you read.** One of the best ways to learn textbook information is to try to outguess the writer. As you preview a chapter's introduction and headings, ask yourself what is likely to be in the chapter. Look for probable test questions that could come from the information. Ask yourself about the order in which the information is presented, and notice techniques the writer uses to emphasize some points over others (such as putting them first or last or in bold print).

6. **Highlight the text and make notes in the margins to emphasize key points.** Use a yellow marking pen to highlight key words or ideas in the text, or pencil notes to yourself in the margin of the text. Do not overuse this method, however, or everything will be emphasized and it will only waste your time. Probably the best **highlighting methods** include the following:

- Divide the reading into sections (if more than five pages).
- Preview an entire section first by skimming through it quickly.
- Once you have familiarized yourself with the contents, read it again slowly and highlight the key points.
- Make notes in the margins using your own words to summarize the main ideas.
- Once completed, review your highlights to make sure they cover all the key concepts you want to remember from the heading.

With this method, you will have a clearer picture of the material and integrate it more fully. You also can review the material more quickly and thoroughly.

7. **Outline the content as you read.** An alternative method to highlighting is to take brief notes of key words and ideas on a separate piece of paper as you read. See if you can understand the structure of the information as you read it. Your outline will be a useful tool for review later in the course.

8. **Learn to increase your speed if you are a slow reader.** If you know you have a problem with speed, a workshop or a session with a study counselor may help you identify techniques for increasing your speed. By working at increasing reading speed, you can improve dramatically.

---

*The SQ3R Method for Studying Texts*

**Survey:**    Preview the information to be studied before reading.

**Question:** Ask yourself critical questions about the content of what you are reading.

**Read:**     Conduct the actual reading in small segments.

**Recite:**    Stop periodically to recite to yourself what you have just read so you know you understand it.

**Review:**    Once you have completed the section, review the main points to make sure you remember them. Review again in a follow-up session.

---

# How to Take Lecture Notes

How do you usually take notes in a lecture class? Do you try to record all the information the instructor presents? Do you listen just for ideas that are not presented in the textbook and keep your notes fairly short? Or do you just listen and try to get the main ideas without letting any note taking distract you?

Just as different instructors use textbooks differently, so also do they give different emphasis and importance to lectures. Some instructors use lectures as a way merely to review and highlight the material in the textbook. Others use lectures to present totally new information that is not to be found in the text. You need to understand the emphasis an instructor will place on lecture information so you will know how to record and study it.

If you are uncertain of how your instructor will test you over lecture materials, ask politely so you will know how detailed your note taking has to be. Some instructors prefer that you merely listen and try to integrate the information given in the lectures. Others want you to master the information and be tested on it in addition to the text material. Knowing the difference will save you time and help you focus your attention during lectures on the information that will be of most value to you.

When you know you will be tested on lecture material, the following suggestions will help you record and study that information more effectively.

1. **Arrive early and stay late.** The most important information in a lecture is often presented in the first two minutes and in the last two minutes of class. Instructors may change assignment due dates, give helpful advice, or make important announcements that you will miss if you come late or leave early. Asking friends to let you review their notes may not get this special information to you. Likewise, not being present for these

announcements will not give you the opportunity to ask clarifying questions.

2. **Do the assigned reading before the lecture.** Instructors often build upon the reading assigned for a lecture and assume that you have read certain information. If you have not read it, you will probably be lost and miss many of the important elements of the lecture.

3. **Prepare a question to ask the instructor.** If you want an instructor to know you are doing the reading, prepare an intelligent question based on your homework. Instructors often ask for questions, and they invariably are met by blank stares from students who have not done the reading or otherwise prepared for the class. You will appear well prepared if you consistently ask good questions that help you thoroughly understand the textbook. Preparing good questions should be a part of your studying for a class, so you can show the instructor you are studying and preparing for lectures by having your questions ready.

4. **Be prepared and systematic.** The following suggestions can help you keep your notes organized. Have fresh paper for each class session. Use the same kind of paper every time. Begin by entering the date so you can keep your notes in order. Use blank pages from a three-ring binder that can be removed during review sessions. Handouts and other class materials can be inserted where they fit into your notes. Keep your notes organized in a folder or binder for the class along with all other materials pertinent to that class.

5. **Look for the structure of a lecture.** Good lecturers will explain the structure of their lectures by providing a preview and dividing the talk into clear parts. Some excellent lecturers even provide an outline of their talk on the chalkboard or in a visual aid for you to follow as they speak. If you are confronted by a poor lecturer, however, you will have to figure out the structure on your own. Listen closely for the main points that help organize the information being presented. If an instructor is exceptionally disorganized, a polite request for an outline or a study guide of main points to help you follow the lecture might prompt him into being a little more structured. The following chart lists the elements of a well-structured lecture.

6. **Look for the main points of the lecture.** Good lecturers will make their main points clear by emphasizing them—by repeating them, or by writing them down, or by stressing them vocally. Listen for these clues, and record this emphasis in your notes. Compare your notes to those of other students in the class and see if you are hearing the same things being emphasized. If a lecture is particularly confusing, visit the instructor during office hours and discuss the problem you are having with your notes. She can clarify the issues you do not understand and will know that you are working hard to

*Elements of a Well-Structured Lecture*

| | |
|---|---|
| **Topic:** | a clear statement of the subject of the lecture |
| **Context:** | how this lecture fits in with what came before and what will come afterward in the class |
| **Parameters:** | what areas will be included and excluded in the lecture, and why these were selected |
| **Preview:** | a pre-summary of the major parts of the lecture |
| **Main Sections:** | division of the lecture into major parts |
| **Details:** | for each main section, the most important details to remember |
| **Transitions:** | the clues that announce when the lecturer moves from one part or point to another |
| **Summaries:** | a repetition of the key points, either occasionally at the end of main sections or at the end of the entire lecture |
| **Test Items:** | suggestions as to which points or details will be on the test |
| **Visual Aids:** | use of the chalkboard, overhead transparencies, a computer slide show program, or handouts to emphasize main points or to clarify details |

understand the information. You might politely make some suggestions about how the lecture could be organized more clearly.

7. **Take notes on only half the page.** As you take notes, leave either the right or the left half of the page blank. When reviewing your notes, use this space to include things you may have missed during the lecture. If you compare notes with a friend or if you compare your lecture notes with your reading, you may see similarities or differences that you want to emphasize. The blank space in your lecture notes will give you the room to highlight these differences. When preparing for exams, you can also use the space to emphasize key words or concepts embedded in your notes. The accompanying illustrations shows one student's method for note taking. Notice the key elements:

- Each page is labeled, numbered, and dated.
- Notes are taken on only one half of the page.
- Space is left between notes for review.
- Key concepts are highlighted.
- Special items are emphasized.
- Questions and points that need clarification are written in the blank space opposite the notes.

## Sample Page from Student Notebook

---

ENGLISH 101                                      p. 23
JAN. 15 (WED.)
"5 Qualities of Effective Writing"

---

| | |
|---|---|
| *Announcement | Quiz on Friday* |
| | |
| 5 Qualities of | |
| Effective Writing | |
| 1. accuracy | |
| 2. clarity | |
| 3. conciseness | |
| 4. appropriateness | |
| 5. dynamism | |
| | |
| These apply to all | |
| types of writing | |
| – letters | |
| – essays | |
| – resumes | Ask – what about |
| – newspaper articles | comic books? |
| – textbooks | Don't they break |
| | all the rules? |
| 1. Accuracy | |
| definition when there | |
| are specific rules for | |
| usage (right + wrong) | |
| – spelling | |
| – grammar | |
| – punctuation | |

---

8. **Review your notes immediately after class.** The best method for mastering the information presented in a lecture is to review your notes immediately after the class. Try to fill in any blanks you may have. Ask yourself critical questions about the information in your notes. Is it clear? Is it related to what you know from the reading? What will probably be on the test? These questions will help you better remember lecture information, and you will have advance preparation for later exams.

9. **Organize your class notes in a binder.** Devise some system for holding class notes, syllabuses, and assignment sheets all together. A large three-ring binder can contain notes from several classes, or you may want to have a separate folder for each class. Whichever system works best for you, get in the habit of keeping all

your class notes together in an organized way. This will help you feel in control of the information, and you will always have it available when you study. You can also keep a small set of office supplies—extra pens, pencils, paper, a small stapler, a pair of scissors, or even a hole puncher—in your folder to help you stay organized.

## Closing Thoughts

A few hours invested in improving your study skills may be one of the best investments of time you can make. Your school may offer workshops on the skills introduced in this chapter. Many books are available to help you more fully develop these skills on your own. There is one important principle to remember, however: Knowing about skills is not the same as being able to use the skills. You have to practice these methods and refine your use of them, and that takes applied effort. Make a concerted effort to use some of the techniques suggested in this chapter and see if they make a difference in your comprehension of course material. For the time you invest, the payoff is great: higher grades, more thorough learning, and greater interest in your classes.

# Reviewing Your Study Techniques

*Instructions: Rate your study habits on the following form. Honestly answer each questions and total your score at the end.*

Scale: (1) Never          (2) Sometimes          (3) Always

1. Do you read some of the text before the first session of class?          1  2  3
2. Do you study hardest the first two weeks of a class?          1  2  3
3. Do you have a regular place to study?          1  2  3
4. Do you have regularly scheduled study times?          1  2  3
5. Do you study mostly during the day?          1  2  3
6. Do you study in many short sessions rather than cramming before exams?          1  2  3
7. Do you regularly use study aids such as test files, study guides, or practice sessions?          1  2  3
8. Do you preview chapters before reading them?          1  2  3
9. Do you read information in a text at least twice?          1  2  3
10. Do you review the information in a text chapter immediately after you have finished it?          1  2  3
11. Do you highlight or take notes when reading texts?          1  2  3
12. Do you ask yourself critical questions as you read?          1  2  3
13. Do you read assigned materials before a class?          1  2  3
14. Do you regularly come to class early?          1  2  3
15. Do you take notes in lecture classes?          1  2  3
16. Do you compare or review your notes after class?          1  2  3
17. Can you tell the difference between a well-structured lecture and a disorganized one?          1  2  3
18. Can you recognize key points when they are made in lectures?          1  2  3
19. Do you have a folder system to organize your notes for each class?          1  2  3
20. Do you set study goals for each class and stick to them?          1  2  3

Total Score _____

Note on scoring: The following scores will give you some
indication of the strength of your study skills.

If you scored:   51 to 60   Your study skills are **excellent.** You should
consider becoming a peer mentor for other
students.

41 to 50   Your study skills are **good** but could use
improvement in some areas.

31 to 40   Your study skills could be stronger. They
require improvement in several areas.

21 to 30   Your study skills could be much stronger.
You should seriously consider extra work
to improve them in all areas.

Based on these results, give close attention to the text as it discusses areas of
study skills that you need to improve.

# EXERCISE 13

## Practicing Highlighting and Making Margin Notes

*Instructions: Read the following essay and highlight in some way the key points that would help you summarize the main points of this essay to your instructor. You may wish to review the suggestions for highlighting and making notes in the chapter before you complete this exercise. Once you have completed the highlighting and margin notes, answer the questions at the end of the exercise.*

## An Essay:
## Ben Franklin's Life Has Lessons For Today's Grads

*by Dr. Eric J. Soares, California State University, Hayward*

What do you share in common with Benjamin Franklin? One thing: ample opportunity to do good work. Franklin made the most of his opportunities. Will you?

We know that Franklin must have been a genius. He discovered the Gulf Stream and principles of electricity. He invented bifocals and the Franklin stove. He invented a musical instrument and played the harp, guitar, and violin. As a swimmer, he could not be beaten. He was a well-rounded person, even in an age of the "Renaissance Man." He made a modest fortune as a printer, writer, editor, and publisher. He drew America's first political cartoon. He designed the first mail-order catalogue. He is the father of American advertising. But that is not all.

Franklin was very civic-minded. The first militia and subscription library in America were started by Franklin. He was Pennsylvania's first governor, America's first postmaster general, an accomplished diplomat, and a courageous patriot. He is the grandfather of our nation.

He died 200 years ago at the age of 84. He accomplished a great deal in his lifetime, yet by the age of 21 he had just learned the trade of printing and was flat broke. He made all his major contributions to life after he mastered his trade and went to work in earnest.

### You Know More Than Ben

You may not be a printer, but you possess something that Franklin never could have—the chance for a college education. In your general education classes you acquire more knowledge than Franklin ever could. Because of people like Franklin, your college education is possible. He furthered the cause of higher education in America. Because of his contributions, you know more facts and theories than Franklin. You have access to more knowledge of science, mathematics, social studies, and literature than the man on the hundred dollar bill.

In addition to acquiring specific and general knowledge, you learn how to solve problems in your local community. You learn critical thinking, logic, and knowing how to know (research methods). You know that when coupled with problem-solving skills, knowledge is real power. But knowledge and problem-solving skills are not enough. As Einstein said, "Imagination is more important than knowledge." You have the opportunity to use your imagination and express your creativity in humanities classes such as art, music, theater, and many other courses.

Knowledge, problem-solving skills, and imagination amply prepare you for success in life, but you are gaining another essential skill in school: oral and written communication. Mastering communication skills allows you to interact effectively with your fellow humans to accomplish great deeds.

So, after you graduate, you will go forth into the world with knowledge (both general and specialized), problem-solving methods, an active and developed imagination, and communication skills. Ben Franklin would admire you. He would respect your college degree because he valued higher education. He came from a poor family and had no money to attend college. He was forced to educate himself. Obviously, he did a good job.

After he earned his fortune through honest effort in the publishing and printing business, Franklin spent years trying to establish a university. In 1749 he succeeded, and the University of Philadelphia was founded. He ensured that a college education was free for poor students. He also set up a trust fund to teach trades to young people. By 1990, Franklin's trust fund had grown to several million dollars. How Franklin solved the education problem in Philadelphia is no mystery. He used knowledge, logic, imagination, and his consummate communication skills to design and execute a pragmatic plan that worked.

### Ample Opportunity Abounds for You

You may think that Franklin had more opportunities for success than you because he lived in a frontier country. It was only frontier for American colonists; native Americans had resided in Pennsylvania for far more than 200 years before Franklin was born. Still, many unique challenges confronted Franklin back in the 1770s. But challenges and opportunities still abound for you today. What are some of these? In California, we face major problems such as AIDS, homelessness, earthquakes and other natural and man-made disasters, traffic congestion, substance abuse, illiteracy, drought, violent crime, and more. Everywhere in America these kinds of problems exist and need solutions. If Franklin were here, he might grapple with these problems. But he is not here—you are. If you do not address these pressing concerns, who will?

Realistically, you probably will not save the world during your first year out of college (but you never know). Most likely, you will land a job after searching for a while. Like Franklin, you will probably start your under-paid job and work long hours doing flunky work for someone else. Eventually, if you work hard, save money, practice frugality, lead a virtuous life, and do everything in moderation, opportunities will arise to improve your situation—so says Franklin. A time will come when you get the opportunity to use the knowledge and skills you have developed at college. The opportunity may come from out of the blue or be created by you. Either way, I guarantee you will get the chance to contribute to life. Just pay attention and take the opportunity when the door opens for you.

Your real education begins the day you leave the university and set out to find your place in life. As your life progresses, you will keep acquiring knowledge, solving problems with logic and imagination, and communicating what you have learned. That is all that Ben Franklin did.

You will not accomplish what Ben accomplished; you will accomplish something unique, something new. Remember, you share one thing in common with Ben Franklin. That's right—ample opportunity to do good work. Franklin made the most of his opportunities. So will you.

*Reprinted by permission of the author.*

*Answer the following questions by referring to the sections of the essay that you highlighted. If you highlighted correctly and made concise margin notes, you should be able to find the answers by looking only at your highlights and margin notes and not having to reread the essay.*

1. In 10 words or fewer, what is the point of the essay?

2. Using short phrases (three or four words), compose an outline of the major elements contained in the essay.

3. What are the four things you gain in college that Franklin would have valued?

4. How are you similar to or different from Franklin in the matter of "opportunity"?

# Analyzing Lecture Techniques

*Instructions: Review the elements of a well-structured lecture as described in this chapter. Observe the lecture techniques of one of your instructors, and critique her lecture methods using the following form.*

Class Observed:

Instructor:

- Which of the techniques suggested in this chapter did the lecturer use to make the information clear, organized, and easy to understand?

- Did the lecturer do anything that inhibited your understanding of the information presented in the lecture?

- What suggestions could you make to the lecturer that might improve your learning in his or her class? Are you willing to make these suggestions? Why, or why not?

# 4

# "Is this going to be on the test?"

This question is not a good one to ask your instructors because it implies that information that is not going to be on a test is less important in the minds of students. On the other hand, it is vitally important for students to know exactly what they will be tested about. Any class contains far more information than is possible to absorb, and students must be able to give their greatest attention to the information that is most central to the course—which is the same information usually on the test. Thus, this is an important question for students to have answered, even if they must figure it out for themselves or ask it in some other form.

Testing is a necessary part of any course. It serves as a form of feedback to students as to how they are mastering the information.

Unfortunately, many students and instructors see testing, and the resulting grading, as a form of reward or punishment. Or worse yet, some students see testing as a personal evaluation of their worth. They feel that they are somehow stupid or lazy if they do poorly on a test. These inaccurate perceptions make testing extremely stressful for some students, and their performance may suffer, even though they might know the information being tested. This is the phenomenon of test anxiety, in which attitudes surrounding the test get in the way of accurately measuring what the student knows. This chapter investigates methods to overcome test anxiety and to make the testing a more accurate measure of actual learning.

Good instructors help students deal with this problem by structuring their testing procedures in a fair and reasonable manner. They try to make their testing a positive feedback experience by explaining the testing procedures in advance, providing clear criteria for how results will be graded, giving students advance notice on what will be included in the test, and providing adequate debriefing after the test so students can learn from the testing procedure. Extremely helpful instructors go even further by providing sample questions to help students prepare, review sessions to cover exceptionally difficult material, or copies of past exams so students can orient themselves to the types of questions that will be asked.

Unfortunately, not all instructors have such enlightened attitudes about testing, nor are they all so helpful as to provide those extra teaching methods. When faced with less helpful instructors, students must employ methods that will help them perform well on tests. Once you have confidence in your test-taking skills, you can give more concentrated attention to the course content. This chapter provides methods in general test-taking skills and gives specific suggestions for multiple-choice, true-false, matching, short-answer, and essay question forms of tests.

## General Test-Taking Skills

The best piece of advice for anyone who wants to pass a test is to study the material well in advance. *Good study skills have no substitutes.* All the testing tricks in the world will not help you if you have not adequately studied the material and prepared for a class. The study skills in Chapter 3 are the best preparation for a test.

On the other hand, if you do study effectively but still do not perform well on tests, the following suggestions will help you reduce anxiety and better prepare for examinations. Sometimes instructors can be influenced to be more helpful. Likewise, investing the time in preparing for exams will help you more thoroughly master the information in a course. Preparing for tests is just another aspect of good study skills.

1. **Anticipate what will be on the test.** As you read textbooks and listen to lectures, constantly ask yourself to identify probable test questions from the material. As you become more familiar with an instructor, you probably will be able to anticipate most of the kinds of information and the types of test questions that will be on an exam. If you have trouble anticipating what will be on a test, create probable test questions, share them with a study buddy, and practice quizzing yourselves to prepare for the test.

2. **Organize the information in a course.** Most courses contain a great deal of information. To master it, you must organize this mountain of facts. Good study techniques should help you get a sense of the big picture in a course and the smaller sections that comprise individual units, sections, chapters, lectures, and assignments. The more you understand the organization of information, the easier it is to remember specific, individual facts.

3. **Use mnemonic devices to remember lists.** Students for centuries have used mnemonic devices to remember difficult lists. For example, the number of days in the months is best remembered by the old saying, "Thirty days hath September, April, June, and November. All the rest have thirty-one—except February alone, which hath but twenty-eight in fine 'til leap year makes it twenty-nine." Other mnemonic devices use the first letter of each word in a list to create a new word or a clever sentence. For example, the lines of the treble clef in music (E, G, B, D, F) are remembered by the saying, "Every Good Boy Does Fine." Create your own devices for lists you encounter in courses.

4. **Review several times before a test.** Distributed study over several review sessions is far better than a single, massive review session immediately before a test. Regularly incorporate review sessions as you study the material in a course.

5. **Use overlearning to master information.** Even the most accomplished pianists continue practicing a sonata once they have learned it. They know that memory erodes and the stress of a performance may cause a memory lapse. Continue to study information even beyond the point of simple recall or recognition. This added study will embed the information in your long-term memory and make it unforgettable.

6. **Study your instructor's testing style.** Every instructor is different in his testing practices. If possible, review prior exams, test questions, and grading practices for assignments. Some instructors will provide these if you ask for them. Most will not give you a direct answer to the question. "What's going to be on the exam?" but will offer helpful suggestions if you have specific questions about the information in a course.

7. **Attend test review sessions.** If your instructor offers review sessions, by all means attend them. She may give sample

questions as well as more specific guidelines as to what will be on the test to those students who put in the extra effort. If your instructor does not offer these, you can create your own with classmates and study buddies by quizzing each other with probable questions.

8. **Build confidence and positive attitudes about testing.** If you are well-prepared for an exam, you will probably do well on it. The more thoroughly you master study and test-preparation skills, the more your test performance will improve. If tests do not accurately reflect your knowledge of course material, discuss this problem with your instructor to see if you can develop methods for overcoming this obstacle. Most instructors want to help you learn, and they do not want their tests to be barriers to your learning, so they will appreciate your concern and effort and try to help you.

9. **Turn fear into an action plan.** If you know you are beset with test anxiety and this impedes your performance, take steps to help conquer this problem. It will not go away if you do nothing; it will only get worse. The best thing to do is to talk to a learning skills counselor to determine the reasons for the anxiety and to find methods for coping with it. If you have tried everything else on your own, you need the help of experts in the matter. Counselors can help you learn to channel this fear into actions steps that will reduce the anxiety.

10. **Use smart test behaviors.** What you do during a test is just as important as the preparation you might have put into studying for the test. The following chart lists suggestions for behavior during the actual test that will help you achieve your potential. Experiment and find the ones that work most effectively for you.

---

*Smart Test-Taking Behaviors*

- Arrive early at the test site.
- Get settled, relax, and give yourself time to organize your thoughts.
- Listen carefully to instructions.
- Read directions thoroughly and make sure you understand exactly what you are supposed to do during the test.
- Review the entire test before starting.
- Plan a schedule for answering questions.
- Note the penalty rules and calculate the best odds for guessing.
- Breathe deeply and rest occasionally during the exam.

11. **Learn from follow-up sessions.** If your instructor offers debriefing sessions after exams, these are the best ways to learn from the testing experience. These sessions will provide information on what you missed, why you erred as you did, and how the instructor thinks. This information will be extremely useful as you plan for your next test with this instructor. Instructors are also more likely to give you the benefit of the doubt about poor questions or alternative answers if you are present to argue your case directly during the review of the test.

## Techniques for Multiple-Choice Questions

Multiple-choice questions are designed to test your memory of specific details. They are constructed with the following parts:

- **stem**—the sentence or phrase that poses a question;
- **right answer**—the element that provides the correct information to the stem question;
- **distractors**—wrong or misleading answers to the stem question.

Distractors can be wrong in several ways. They often contain information that is the exact opposite of the correct answer. Distractors may also contain only partial information, or they contain both correct and incorrect informative elements. Finally, some distractors are totally irrelevant to the information asked for in the stem. Knowing the way in which multiple-choice questions are constructed will help you understand the logic behind the question and your answer choices.

Knowing the subject matter thoroughly has no substitute. Adequate study in preparation for a multiple-choice exam will make you more confident and likely to score high on the exam. Even with adequate preparation, however, you can increase your chances of finding right answers if you follow these suggestions.

1. **Come to the exam with extra materials.** Bring extra pens, pencils, and scratch paper to the test site. You never know when you might need a back-up pencil or paper to do calculations or to help out friends who forgot theirs.

2. **Review the entire exam.** Note the number and types of questions asked in the exam. Calculate the time you have for each section, and estimate a schedule so you will have enough time to complete all sections.

3. **Record your answers neatly.** Take special care to be extremely neat and precise in recording your responses on the answer sheet. Smudges or incomplete erasures often disqualify an answer.

4. **Work through the test slowly, calmly, and methodically.** Occasional brief rest breaks will help you maintain your concentration and control stress. Breathing deeply and relaxing your tense muscles will increase your memory recall.

5. **Answer the easy questions first.** As you work through the exam, do not get bogged down by a difficult question. If it will take time to analyze and find the answer, move on to easier questions and come back to the difficult ones after you have completed the rest of the exam. Take care not to get your answers out of order on the answer sheet if you skip questions.

6. **Read the stem question and answers thoroughly.** Even though you think you see the correct answer immediately, take the time to read the stem and try each answer. Test the information in each of the answers to determine why it is in error. This should help you eliminate the incorrect answers and verify the right one. Tricky questions are best uncovered with this technique.

7. **Know the penalty for guessing.** If the instructor penalizes wrong choices, it is better to leave an answer blank unless you can narrow down the choices to two. If there is no penalty for guessing, it is best always to select an answer, even if you have no clue as to the correctness of the choices.

8. **Use the process of elimination to make guesses.** When you are not certain of the correct answer, try to eliminate the answers you know are wrong. This will increase your chances of selecting the right answer if you have to guess. The odds are better if you can narrow down the correct answer to one of two choices. This is the process of "educated guessing."

9. **Determine if the test is instructor-created.** Instructors who compose their own questions are usually not as systematic as computer-generated or testing-service testers. When an instructor has composed his test, the following clues may point to the right answer:

   - The longest answer may be the correct one.
   - Middle answers tend to be correct more often.
   - Correct answers will agree with the stem in indefinite article (*a* or *an*), number (singular or plural), and pronoun gender.
   - Qualifiers (such as *sometimes, may, could*) usually point to correct answers.
   - Absolutes (such as *always, never, all*) usually are incorrect.
   - Exactly opposite answers usually indicate that one of them is the correct answer.
   - Silly or humorous answers are often incorrect.

10. **Look for inter-question clues.** The information provided in a stem may help you answer another question on the test. Keep an eye open for clues that will help you find the correct answer in a different question.

11. **If a question is confusing, ask for clarification.** Instructors sometimes compose ambiguous or vague questions. Asking for clarification will draw their attention to the problem, and you may get more information to help you find the right answer. If you are certain the question is a poor one, collect your evidence and politely talk with the instructor after the exam. Such effort shows that you are a serious and careful student.

12. **Review your answer sheet once you are done.** At the end of the exam, review the answer sheet to make sure you have answered all questions. You can also go over each question to make sure you have not erred in recording the answer. In general, it is best not to change answers unless you are absolutely sure you made a wrong choice. First choices are most often the correct ones unless you overlooked some clue in the distractors.

## Techniques for True-False Questions

True-false questions are similar to multiple-choice ones. The major difference is that you have only two choices. Most of the techniques discussed for multiple-choice questions apply to true-false questions as well. Below are the most important suggestions to remember.

1. **Read the question closely.** Try to understand the deeper implications of what the question is asking so you can defend in your own mind the correctness of your choice.

2. **Look for multiple parts in a question.** A question may have several elements of information. To be true, all elements in the question must be true. To be false, only one element has to be false.

3. **Be careful with multiple negatives.** Translate questions with double negatives into positive terms. For example, the question "No birds are without feathers" is more confusing than the question "All birds have feathers." If a question has a triple negative, ask the instructor for clarification.

4. **Qualifiers usually point to true answers.** Words such as *often, usually, seldom, many, most, few, generally, typically, may,* or *could* tend to make answers more inclusive and, therefore, more likely true.

5. **Absolutes usually point to false answers.** Words such as *always, never, all, none, invariably, must,* or *have to* tend to make answers more exclusive and, therefore, more likely false.

6. **Instructor-created answers tend to be true.** Instructors want to impart correct information, so they more likely will pose questions positively. If you are totally uncertain of an answer, and there is no penalty for guessing, a true choice is more likely correct.

# Techniques for Matching Lists

Test components that ask you to match two lists are challenges to keep many similar facts organized and clear. They are used most often to match concepts with examples, terms with definitions, events with dates, or generalities with specific details. Matching questions consist of a question list that serves as the stem and an answer list that serves as the pool of possible responses.

The following suggestions will help you to organize the information you do know and to avoid confusion in a matching question.

1. **Determine if the lists are exclusive.** In an exclusive list, each element in the question list must be matched with an element in the answer list. Thus, all elements in the answer list should be used. The instructor may not be willing to tell you if the lists are exclusive, but it will not hurt to ask. If the lists are not exclusive, then you know you can use an answer more than once.

2. **Review both lists first.** Familiarize yourself with the contents of both lists. This will help you avoid confusing similar elements in the lists.

3. **Match answers with the correct questions.** It is often easier to select an answer and then try to find the correct question. Answer stems are sometimes easier to identify than the question stems.

4. **Match the elements you are certain of first.** This technique helps you eliminate the number of possible answers left in the pool. In an exclusive list you can check off answers and questions as you use them, thus reducing the chances of making incorrect matches.

# Techniques for Short-Answer Questions

Short-answer questions consist of an incomplete stem that you must complete by filling in the blank or responding with a word or phrase. The questions often test your knowledge of vocabulary or specific facts. They can also serve as a "mini-essay" in which you must pack several specific facts to make a complete answer.

The following techniques will help you more effectively complete this sort of question.

1. **Read the question closely.** Attend to key words and ideas in the stem question to jog your memory of specific details from your reading or the lecture. Most questions are looking for specific details in the answer, so try to figure out what the question is looking for.

2. **Use key words or instructor's key ideas to answer.** Questions often ask for specific technical terms or ideas the instructor has emphasized in the class. Recall the words the instructor used in lecture and use them to frame your answer.

3. **Pack your answer with several specific facts.** Unless the question is obviously looking for one key word or idea, pack several specific details into your answer. It is better for your answer to have too much information than not enough. This technique is called telescoping, packing facts together for greater effect.

4. **Word the answer precisely.** Use concrete terms and specific facts rather than vague generalities. This is especially important when you are not certain of the exact answer. The more precise your answer is, the more likely it will be given credit.

5. **Ask for clarification when you have alternative answers.** Some short-answer questions can be answered in several different ways. If you must choose between answers you know are correct, ask the instructor in general terms for the best way to answer the question. For example, the question "Most hogs are raised in the United States in _____" could be answered either by a state (Iowa) or a region (the Midwest). You could ask your instructor, "Do you want the state or the region?" to clarify and avoid making a wrong choice.

6. **Look for agreement clues in the question stem.** Short-answer questions often contain clues as to number, gender, or first letter. The following examples demonstrate these clues:

   - Maine's major exports are _____. (The answer should contain at least two elements because of the plural stem.)
   - The first national celebrity to make his illness public before dying of AIDS was _____. (The answer is a man because of the pronoun.)
   - Andy Warhol's greatest claim to fame is his contributions as an _____. (The answer will start with a vowel because of the article clue.)

7. **Watch for space clues.** When a question has a blank for you to fill in, clues are sometimes embedded in the length of the space or the number of spaces provided. The following examples demonstrate these clues:

   - The Confederation of American States had _____ members. (The answer is a number because the small blank is provided.)
   - The 40th President of the United States was _____ _____. (The best answer is first and last name because two blanks are provided.)

# Techniques for Writing Essay Exam Answers

Essay exam questions are a good test of your writing skill. Many students are frustrated by essay exams because they think they know the information the test covers but they are not confident about their ability to put into writing what they know. Although it is necessary to know the content of the answer, you must also know how to write your answer in a way that will demonstrate your knowledge.

The first skill is to familiarize yourself with essay jargon—key terms in essays that should direct the flow of your thoughts as you plan your answer. See the box on the following page for helpful essay terms and methods for framing an answer.

The following suggestions will help you to plan and write answers to essay exam questions that are thorough and on the mark.

1. **Prepare for the exam.** Anticipate the kinds of questions that will be asked on the exam. Ask to see samples of good answers if your instructor is willing to share them. Write your own questions that you expect to be on the exam. Prepare answers to expected questions in advance and critique them with a study buddy. Memorize key facts that will strengthen essay answers.

2. **Practice your essay writing skills.** If you know you have a weakness in the area of essay exam answers, practice this skill before you take your next exam. If your campus has a study center or a writing center, these resources usually offer workshops or tutoring on how to write essays more effectively. Many English departments offer courses and workshops on essay writing. If nothing else is available, you can design your own workshop—and perhaps offer it to other students who want to learn this skill—by practicing answer writing on questions from old exams. Use the following suggestions to improve your essay writing and critique your practice answers with friends. Find a friend who has the skills of essay writing and analyze his methods. (The trouble with this technique, however, is that many people cannot articulate exactly how they perform the skill—they do it intuitively without knowing exactly how they do it.)

3. **Plan your answers systematically.** When confronted with an essay exam, the first step, as with any writing project, is to plan carefully. Schedule your time so you will have enough time for each answer you have to write. If you have a choice among questions to answer, select those you feel most confident about. Take a few minutes at the beginning of the exam to organize your thoughts so you will not jumble your facts or forget things that are important to include. As you write your answers, keep track of the time so you do not run out of time for the last few questions.

4. **Follow exam instructions carefully.** Look for directions on how to select questions, whether to write on both sides of the

### Key Terms in Essay Questions

**Comment:** The same as "discuss."

**Compare:** Show the similarities between two things. It is best to do this in a logical order with a clear organizational structure.

**Contrast:** Show the differences between two things. Be systematic in organizing your points.

**Critique:** (also called "criticize" or "evaluate") Take a position on the value of an idea and provide arguments that support your opinion. The instructor is looking here for evidence, not just your opinion, so be sure to focus on specific facts and details, not just generalities.

**Define:** Give a definition of a term or concept. The best way to define is to give the general category and then the specific features that make the concept unique. To expand an answer, you can use comparison or contrast to show how the idea is similar to or different from other related ideas.

**Demonstrate:** The same as "prove."

**Discuss:** (also called "describe" or "explain") Give a complete picture of an idea or situation. This is the most difficult essay question because you can include many different things. Organize your thoughts by using key words such as *background, overview, development, cause and effect, results, conclusion, future trends,* or whatever is appropriate to the answer.

**Illustrate:** Provide an example or a specific application of an idea or a concept.

**Outline:** (also called "list" or "summarize") Put in outline form the key ideas or main points of a concept. Make the outline look like an outline—complete with main points and subpoint headings.

**Prove:** (also called "support" or "defend") Show that an idea is true or false by means of arguments and evidence that support those arguments. The best technique here is to have a few main arguments and to organize your specific facts underneath each argument. Include specific details to support your ideas.

**Trace:** A discussion in a historical framework. Names and dates are important factors in this answer.

page, whether to write in ink or pencil, whether to double-space your answer, or whatever. If you have any questions about writing your answers, have them clarified by the instructor before you begin writing.

5. **Outline your answers before you begin.** Before you start to write on each answer, carefully outline the main points you want to include in your answer. Jot down key facts, figures, or dates that are pertinent and will strengthen your answer. Do not spend a great deal of time outlining, because you need to spend most of your time writing. But a few minutes spent on an outline will make your answers much more complete and logically organized, and therefore stronger.

6. **Begin the answer with a strong statement that takes a specific position.** You want to begin your answer with a forceful statement that clearly commits you to a specific position on the question. A poor technique is to equivocate by taking a neutral or ambiguous position on an answer. Most instructors interpret this approach as a "snow job." Do not begin with a broad overview or general picture. Get to the specifics, because that is usually what the instructor is looking for in a good answer.

7. **Support your opening position with specific facts.** Once you have taken a position, support it with arguments and specific evidence. This is where your facts and figures come into play. Organize your support into several main points (the body of the essay), and pack your arguments with specific data that demonstrate your knowledge of the material being tested. Avoid vague generalities and unsupported opinions and feelings. Include your personal opinions only if the question specifically asks for them.

8. **Use transitions to show your organization.** Instructors get tired of reading essays; and if you can make yours easier to read, you might get a higher grade. One of the best techniques to make your writing easy to read is the use of transitions. Include a pre-summary in the introduction to forecast the main points of the body of the answer. Use clear transitions as you move from one main point to another. Write clear thesis sentences that demonstrate your organizational structure. Announce supporting elements, such as examples or contrasting arguments, by name as you include them in your answer. These writing signposts make it easy to see the structure of your answer—something most readers appreciate.

9. **Be complete and concise.** Plan your answers to include everything you think the instructor wants to see, but do not run on and on once you have made your point. It does no good to "fake it" by rambling on without specific facts to support your main points. Thus, your answers should be complete, including all specific facts relevant to your answer, but also concise—clearly orga-

nized and to the point. Try to balance both conciseness and completeness in your answer.

10. **Use the instructor's key words and key ideas.** Most instructors have favorite ways of saying things and key points they want to make in a course. As you take notes and study a course, watch for these key words and ideas. Include them in your essay exam answers to show you have been listening. Present the idea in your own words so you are not just repeating back what the instructor has said. Demonstrate that you understand the full impact of the idea by supporting it with your own insights or specific facts.

11. **Make your test form look good.** A good-looking answer is just as important as a smart one. Many instructors grade down answers that are hard to read. Therefore, take care to write neatly and legibly. Take a little extra time to be neat. If the choice is left up to you, double-space your answers and write on only one side of the page. Leave wide margins—especially on the left side of the page—so the instructor can write comments. Indent paragraphs or triple-space between them so that thesis sentences are clearly highlighted. Number the main points if you have a list of them. Write in erasable ink; it looks neater and more confident than pencil. If you have to erase, do so neatly and cleanly.

12. **Before you finish, proofread your answers.** Once you have completed the body of the exam answer, read through your answer to catch any misspellings, incorrect punctuation, or words you have left out (as often happens when people are writing quickly). Also look for any last-minute additions you can include in the conclusion. One or two extra ideas—especially if they are important ones—tacked onto the conclusion will not hurt your organizational plan. Such careful attention to detail shows that you are trying to be thorough. Complete the answer with a conclusion that reiterates the position you took in the introduction and ends on a strong note. Finally, place your name prominently at both the beginning and the end of the essay.

13. **Make only positive personal comments to an instructor.** Some students use essay exams as an opportunity to make personal comments to an instructor about the course. It is probably best not to do that, but if you do, say only positive things. Any negative feedback you might want to convey to an instructor should be done separately. Negative comments may unconsciously affect the way the instructor reads your answer.

## Closing Thoughts

There is no substitute for adequate preparation for exams. There are no secret techniques that will help you succeed in an exam for which you have not adequately studied and prepared yourself. Exam-taking "guessing gimmicks" will help you in only a small number of questions. Doing the required work in a class is your best insurance for good test performance, so prepare carefully and use the techniques suggested in this chapter only as a last resort.

# Analyzing An Instructor's Testing Techniques

*Instructions:* *By now you probably have had an exam in one of your classes. Observe the testing techniques of an instructor in one of your classes by answering the following questions.*

Class Observed:

1. How clearly did the instructor explain in advance what would be on the test? How accurate was that information?

2. How did the instructor help you prepare for the test? Were study aids (such as sample questions, old exams, study guides, review sheets, or review sessions) offered to you?

3. Did the instructor explain the testing procedure on the day of the exam? Were the instructions clear and useful?

4. How helpful was the instructor during the actual test? What did the instructor do to make the test procedure comfortable and unthreatening?

5. Were the grading criteria for the test results explained clearly? Were grades fairly distributed?

6. Did the instructor offer a debriefing session to go over the test results? How effective was this session?

7. What could you do to help your instructor be a more effective and helpful test-giver?

# Answering Multiple-Choice Questions

*Instructions:* *Time to take a test! You may not know anything about the subject, but you will be able to figure out the right answers by using the guidelines suggested for guessing in this chapter. Select the best answer for each of the following questions. After each question, write down the clue that helped you select your answer. You can assume that this is an instructor-created test and that there is no penalty for wrong answers.*

1. Which of the following was most influential in the creation of fencing as a martial art?

   a. swords as court dress

   b. the need for gentlemen to defend themselves in battle and in duels

   c. the invention of gunpowder

   d. the use of armor

   Clue:

2. Which of the following is not a modern fencing weapon:

   a. sabre              c. dirk

   b. epee               d. foil

   Clue:

3. Which of the following parries protects the head?

   a. parry 4          c. parries 2 and 3

   b. parry 6          d. parry 5

   Clue:

4. The most important pieces of protective equipment are:

   a. the mask            c. the underarm shield

   b. the glove and mask    d. anything the fencer wears

   Clue:

5. In sabre fencing, what constitutes the fair target area?

   a. the head only       c. the torso only

   b. the arms only       d. anything from the waist up

   Clue:

6. A weapon most like the original dueling sword is an

   a. epee              c. foil

   b. sabre            d. all the above

   Clue:

7. If parry 5 protects the head, which parries protect the chest?

    a. parry 7               c. parry 2

    b. parries 4 and 6     d. parry 3

    Clue:

8. Which of the following is the main reason for learning to fence?

    a. you never get injured     c. you always have fun doing it

    b. it is a good general workout     d. you can pretend to be Zorro the
                                               Gay Blade

    Clue:

9. All fencing lore originated in France.
    T  F

    Clue:

10. Most fencing is done in Europe.
    T  F

    Clue:

11. No fencers can compete without a face mask.
    T  F

    Clue:

12. Both men and women can compete in foil, but only men can compete in sabre events.
    T  F

    Clue:

*Answers:*  *1. b (longest answer)*                *8. b (a and c absolute,*
          *2. c (middle answer, internal clues-#6)*       *d is silly answer)*
          *3. d (inter-question clues-#7)*           *9. F (absolute)*
          *4. b (plural agreement)*              *10. T (qualifier)*
          *5. d (absolutes)*                   *11. T (double negative)*
          *6. a (article agreement)*             *12. F (two parts, second is*
          *7. b (plural agreement)*                 *absolute)*

## EXERCISE 17

# Answering Short-Answer Questions

*Instructions: Each of the short-answer questions below gives two possible correct answers. Determine which of the answers you think is the better, and state your reasons for selecting it by pointing out the clues in the questions.*

1. What was the cause of the American Civil War?
   A: Although most sources agree that the states' rights to secede from the Union was the precipitating factor in the outbreak of the war, hostilities were heightened by disagreements over slavery and economic competition between North and South.
   B: The states' rights to secede from the Union.

   Reason:

2. What was the most important cause of the American Civil War?
   A: There is no single most important cause to the war, since it was precipitated by the states' rights to secede from the Union but also influenced by the slavery issue and regional economic competition.
   B: States' rights to secede from the Union.

   Reason:

3. How many casualties were incurred in the Civil War?
   A: The Civil War caused the highest death rate of any war fought by the U.S.
   B: More than 450,000 combatants were killed, and millions were wounded, though no accurate records were kept of the wounded. Civilian casualties were likewise not recorded, but estimates range in the millions.

   Reason:

4. The final surrender was signed at _____  _____.
   A: Appomatox
   B: Appomatox Courthouse

   Reason:

5. John Wilkes Booth is mainly known for his role as an _____.
   A: assassin
   B: tragedian

   Reason:

6. Though some called U.S. Grant a great general, who would you nominate as the best Northern general of the war?
   A: Grant, because, in spite of what his critics say, he was able to finally win the war, a feat no other general had been able to do.
   B: Grant was widely criticized for incurring enormous casualties and squandering resources. I would nominate Sherman as the ablest Northern general because of his superior control of logistics and supply problems. He also was the author of the drive to divide the South, thus leading to its ultimate defeat.

   Reason:

7. The key Union victories of July, 1863, were _____.
   A: Gettysburg and Vicksburg
   B: Gettysburg

   Reason:

8. The Battle of Antietam was fought in _____.
   A: 1862
   B: Western Maryland

   Reason:

*Answers:*

*1A.  It telescopes more information together to answer a general question.*

*2B.  The question asks for a single answer. It is best not to argue with the question.*

*3B.  It is packed with specific details which answer the question directly.*

*4B.  There are two blank spaces; the answer should have two words.*

*5A.  The article "an" suggests the answer will start with a vowel.*

*6B.  There seems to be an implied bias against Grant in the way the question is asked. It probably reflects a pet idea of the instructor.*

*7A.  The question asks for two distinct answers even though only one blank is provided.*

*8.  Either A or B. Both are correct and the question does not ask for a date or a location. You should ask the instructor which one she wants answered by the question.*

# 5

## "What's in the library besides books?"

The campus library can be one of your best friends or one of your worst enemies. How would you like to have a friend who could introduce you to new careers, undreamed-of lifestyles, unique hobbies, solutions to problems you face, and interesting information of all sorts? On the other hand, what kind of friend would waste your time, frustrate your efforts to find information you need, and promise all sorts of rewards but never share them with you? The library can be either of these. It all depends on whether you know the kinds of resources available in the library and how to find them when you need them.

The ability to do effective research quickly is an often-overlooked skill in college success. Many students take the library for granted and never learn the skills necessary to do complete and speedy research. Thus, when they are forced to use the library for a term paper or project, they become frustrated and demoralized by the difficulties they encounter. This chapter will introduce you to the basic skills you need to do effective research in an efficient and time-saving manner. Once you have developed these skills, you will use them throughout your entire life as you need information for work, personal interests, or other school-related assignments.

## The Big Problem: Intimidation

Most people are intimidated by the vast amount of information in a library, especially a large academically oriented college library. The seemingly endless rows and rows of books appear to be a huge, cavernous, bottomless pit. If you do not have good research skills, you will likely get that sinking feeling of being overwhelmed by too much information that still does not satisfy your specific needs.

The trick to using the library effectively is to understand the system by which the information in it is organized. All libraries are organized according to a systematic and logical pattern. By clarifying the organizing system and familiarizing yourself with the kinds of information available, you will be able to attack the problem more confidently. Once you understand how the library is organized, you need to develop the shortcut skills to finding things quickly. The two major skills involved are (1) knowing what is in the library and (2) knowing how to find what you need.

If you spend the time to learn the basic skills of library research, they will pay off handsomely later in your school and work career. By committing yourself to learning these skills, you can overcome any anxiety or intimidation you might feel about the library and turn it into one of the best college friends you have ever found.

## What the Library Has to Offer

The first step in library skill is learning what your local library has in it and where these resources are located. Most libraries have **orientation tours** for just this purpose. Spend an hour on one of these tours and you will save countless hours later. Some libraries also offer special workshops, audio- or videotape orientations, computer search instruction programs, brochures, or maps that help orient the new student to the library. Staff people generally are eager to assist students in orienting themselves to the resources. You have to take the initiative, however, and take advantage of this assistance. A bit of time is required, but a good orientation will save you much trouble later.

The following elements are the major components of the library with which you should be familiar. Arrange an orientation tour of your library and locate each of them. In each area spend several minutes familiarizing yourself with what is contained there. Exercise 19 asks you to find these resources in your local library.

**On-line catalogues.** Most college libraries have computerized their holdings. While old card catalogues comprising many drawers may still remain in some libraries, the cards probably have not been updated for several years. Current materials, those holdings purchased within the last few years, will not be included in the card catalogue system. The on-line (or computerized) catalogue lists every book, magazine, newspaper, recording, clipping file, pamphlet, audiotape, videotape, musical score, and picture that the library owns.

The library staff usually provides orientation on how to use the on-line catalogue in order to find what you need. Although the information on the computer screen may be displayed in a manner that is unique to each library, most systems allow you to search by author name, publication title, key words in a title, and Library of Congress subject headings. Some on-line catalogues also allow you to search for materials held on reserve, to place a hold on a particular book, and to review your circulation record. Some systems allow you to access the catalogues of other libraries or research services. Because each system is different, most on-line catalogues provide a "Help" or "Information" key. Pressing this key enables you to bring up a screen that provides instructions on how to use that particular system.

Some libraries make it possible for you to conduct an on-line search without going to the library. Conducting the preliminary search from your computer at home helps you save time because you can determine if the materials you need are available at the library and are on the shelf. To take advantage of this kind of search, you will need a modem. Also, you should check to be certain that your system is compatible with the library's system. If it is, you will probably need to set up an account and choose a password. Check with the librarian for information about conducting searches from your home computer.

**Information desks.** Typically located near the front door is an information desk with a library staff person who can assist you if you are having trouble in the library. Most librarians want to be helpful (though they are often overwhelmed by the number of people who need help), so do not hesitate to ask for assistance if you have tried finding something but cannot locate it. It is probably a good idea to try to find things on your own first and then ask for help only if you get stumped. As you develop your library skills, you will need help less and less. You may even be able to assist your friends in their research tasks.

**Reference room.** Some library resources are so heavily used (and expensive to replace if lost) that they are housed in a special section, usually called the reference room. Encyclopedias, indexes, directories, bibliographies, clipping files, atlases, handbooks, and dictionaries are kept there and are not ever checked out to individuals. You must use them in the reference room. This room is usually a great mystery to beginning researchers, so take 15 minutes one day and just browse the shelves of the reference room in your library to familiarize yourself with the contents. You will be amazed at the wealth of data and research assistance. The resources of the reference room are included in the card catalogues and are marked with the special designation "Ref" or "R."

**Reserve rooms.** Many college libraries provide a service by which faculty members can put materials on reserve so students can read or study them outside of class. Most on-line catalogues provide a list of materials that have been placed on reserve. Lists are usually organized by course title or instructor name. These materials usually can be checked out for a limited time. Because each library is different, explore your library's policy.

**Special indexes.** An index is a listing of articles contained in magazines or journals, often called periodicals because they come out periodically (e.g., once a month). Bound indexes are available on the shelves in a central location, typically near the reference materials. On-line indexes usually are available in specialized databases organized by subject area. Indexes vary from rather general and popular (such as the *Reader's Guide to Periodical Literature,* which contains titles of popular magazines of general interest) to highly specialized professional and academic research findings. As your research becomes more sophisticated and professionally related, you will need to use these special indexes more and more to find highly specialized information sources. It takes extra effort to learn to use these indexes, but they are your best guide to finding information in periodicals.

**Periodical holdings.** Magazines, professional journals, and newspapers are often grouped together in a special location for convenience. The indexes to these sources may not be in the same location, so you need to orient yourself on how the system works in your library. Some libraries offer on-line searches of periodicals. These services include InfoTrack, Lexus/Nexus, and Academic Abstracts. Every library is different in how it catalogues and stores its periodicals. Libraries also have different systems for letting you use them. Spend 15 minutes learning the system in your library. It is also interesting to browse through the periodical holdings (if your library allows access to the stacks) to see the great variety of things available for your research.

**Special holdings.** Most libraries have special collections or documents located in unusual places. For example, *Books in Print,* a useful catalogue of all books currently for sale by publishers, is often placed on a work counter. Historical documents, rare books, local newspapers, current periodicals, a browsing collection, and highly used books may also be located in odd places. If you cannot find a resource, ask the librarian where it might be located.

**Special sections.** Many libraries specialize in certain types of holdings (e.g., law, architecture, music, business, maps, children's literature, films). If it has an unusually large number of sources, the library may group them in a special location. Familiarize yourself with the special sections in your library or the additional locations in other buildings across campus or town that might be of interest to you.

**Separate libraries.** Some libraries are so large that they create entirely separate buildings for special subjects. Often academic departments have a specialized library in their particular subject matter for use by their students and faculty, separate from the large campus library. Likewise, large cities may have specialized-use libraries (such as a business library or one specializing in original historical sources). Often, these special libraries have their own on-line catalogues. Individual faculty members also often have their own personal libraries, which are highly specialized in their particular interest area, from which they may allow you to borrow. Knowing about these unique resources will help you find specialized information.

**Internet access.** You may conduct research through many of the web sites on the Internet. Some libraries provide Internet access.

**Study areas.** Some libraries have specially designated study areas, group discussion rooms, study carrels in which you can leave materials you will be using on a long-term basis, or other special-purpose rooms. If you have unusual research or study needs, check with reference librarians to see how they can help you find what you need.

**Researcher services.** More and more libraries are expanding their services to assist researchers. Some libraries have copy centers, typing rooms, computer information search services, cafeterias, or other services. A tour of your library usually includes an introduction to these services.

# How to Find Information in the Library

Once you know about the kinds of information sources in the library, you need to have the skills to find these sources when you need them. Make no mistake—research is hard work! Good research requires many hours of persistent, painstaking labor. If you apply good research skills, however, the results of all this work will be high-quality information for use in whatever your project might be. Efficient research skills will allow you to use your time wisely and not waste it on dead ends.

The following skills will assist you in doing research quickly and effectively. You may have some of them already, and you may need to develop others. The exercises at the end of this chapter will give you some practice in honing these skills, but their best use would be in an actual research project you are doing. Keep these skills in mind as you do research for a class project or term report.

1. **Clarify your purpose.** The more time you spend analyzing your purpose for doing research, the better the results will be. If you know exactly what you are looking for, you can usually find it (or at least find out that it is not available) in your library. Most beginning researchers make the mistake of starting their research by browsing without a plan. This results in much wasted time. If you are doing research that someone else will evaluate (such as a term paper for a class), spend time with the evaluator to clarify your purpose before you begin research. By doing this, you will have a better idea of what to look for. The evaluator may even be able to give you suggestions about where to look.

2. **Focus your topic carefully.** The biggest difficulties beginning researchers face are either "I can't find anything on my topic" or "There is too much information on my topic." These problems happen because the topic is not focused well. Topics vary in how broad or narrow they are. For example, "Dogs" is an extremely broad topic, and "How to Breed Sheepdogs in California for Fun and Profit" is an extremely narrow topic. As a researcher, you need to be able to broaden or narrow your topic in order to find or limit the information available. If you start with a topic that is too focused, you may have trouble finding information. Broadening your topic will introduce you to sources that will provide important background information on your topic. By beginning with encyclopedias, textbooks and magazines, you will gain a wider perspective. You can then narrow your topic from a range of choices and select information more critically. This strategy will be especially helpful with on-line searches. A very broad, general search is likely to produce an extensive list of materials that you do not have sufficient time to investigate. Narrowing your search will give you a shorter list of sources that are related directly to your topic. This entire process depends upon the researcher's purpose and scope, but the process of broadening or narrowing helps to control the amount of information available. Exercise 18 at the end of this chapter gives you practice in this skill.

3. **Find the right "key word."** Information in libraries is listed in catalogue systems by means of two key word systems. One system of headings was created by the United States Library of Congress. These key word headings are explained in the bound volume *Library of Congress Subject Headings.* This resource is in almost every library. If you do not find the right key word in the subject catalogue to guide you to information you need, check the *Library of Congress Subject Headings* for alternative key words. You may just be looking under the wrong word. This guide also gives related subject headings, narrower and broader subject headings, and other useful suggestions.

Another system of key words is usually available through an on-line catalogue search. That system checks all of the library's holdings for materials that include in their titles the words that you selected. The search also extends to related words and forms of the words that you chose. This sort of key word or title search usually yields more entries than a *Library of Congress Subject Heading* search because of its broader scope. On-line catalogue searches are discussed in more detail later in this chapter.

4. **Ask for help, but do what you can first.** Reference librarians are willing to help, but you should ask for their help only after you have done everything you can on your own. If you are totally stumped, show the librarian what you have done already and then ask where else you might look for information. If you have a topic problem (you don't know what your purpose is) or a focus problem (too broad or too narrow), the librarian may not be able to help you. These are issues you have to resolve before you begin the research.

5. **Keep notes as you research.** As you do research, keep a systematic record of authors, titles, publishers, dates, cities of publication, page numbers, and quotations or facts you might use in the final product. You will need all this information for complete footnotes and bibliographies in papers, so keep it as you go along rather than having to find it all again at the last minute. There are many different note-keeping systems (three-by-five note cards, legal-size pads, etc.), so find one that is comfortable for you and use it systematically to stay organized. If you use an on-line system that allows you to print source information, print selectively so that you do not become overwhelmed by extraneous material. Also, always be certain to include the full citation for all of the materials that your search yields.

6. **Interview the experts.** As you become knowledgeable in your area of research, it is helpful to share what you know with local experts (your instructors are often good for this) to see if you are on the right track and if they can make any suggestions about where else to look for data. As with the reference librarian, the more you know in advance, the more valuable your time with the

expert will be. An expert can tell right away whether you have done the preliminary background work to orient yourself to the topic. If you have done it, the expert is usually glad to be of help. If you have not done your homework, however, the expert knows you are just wasting her time and will not be too eager to cover information you should be able to find on your own.

7. **Constantly be on the lookout for information.** Good research cannot be done in a single sitting. Veteran researchers know they have to approach a project from a long-range perspective. Taking your time allows you to think about your topic, evaluate the information you are finding, talk to people about what you have found so far, browse through bookstores or library shelves to find unexpected sources, and generally just let the information percolate. Keep in mind that some on-line databases require anywhere from 15 to 60 days to update information. An article about your research topic that appeared in your local newspaper yesterday may not be available on-line for several weeks, if at all. Also, not all periodicals are included in all databases that are available on college campuses. You might need to review the latest print editions of some sources for current material. A long-term approach to research makes for deep-level learning and mastery of the subject matter—and better research results. When doing research, give yourself plenty of time.

## How to Conduct an On-Line Catalogue Search

The on-line catalogue is a valuable tool for locating resources. Since on-line systems at various colleges and universities may dif-

```
Type the letter for the way you want to search:
Author, Title, Word, etc.
A > AUTHOR
T > TITLE
Y > AUTHOR/TITLE search
W > WORDS in TITLES and SUBJECTS
S > SUBJECT HEADING
C > CALL NO. & BROWSING
R > RESERVE Lists
I > INFORMATION and your SUGGESTIONS
B > CONNECT to other resources
P > Repeat PREVIOUS Search
V > VIEW your circulation record
D > DISCONNECT
Choose one (A, T, Y, W, S, C, R, I, B, P, V, D)
```

fer, it is important that you become familiar with the on-line catalogue at your school. On-line catalogues may offer different types of specialized searches based on the library's holdings. Several types of searches are common to most on-line systems. The first screen that you see when conducting an on-line catalogue search will probably be similar to this sample.

Notice that you may begin several different types of searches by entering a code letter.

**Author search.** Use an author search if you know the name of the author of the resource(s). After choosing the appropriate code for an author search, you will receive additional instructions.

```
                        AUTHOR:

    Type LAST NAME first, for example → Walker, Alice

                      or just → Walker

    . . . then press the RETURN key
```

Follow the instructions and type the name of the author whose works you would like to locate. Then perform the additional command such as pressing the "Return" or "Enter" key. You will bring up a new screen that lists all of the authors with the name that you entered.

```
    You searched for the AUTHOR:  walker alice
    2 AUTHORS found, with 24 entries;  AUTHORS 1-2 are:

        1      Walker Alice       5 entries
        2      Walker Alice 1944 19 entries

    Please type the NUMBER of the item you want to
    see, OR
    N > NEW Search        D > DISPLAY Title,
    A > ANOTHER Search        Locations and Call #
    by AUTHOR             L > LIMIT this Search
    P > PRINT
    Choose one (1-2, N, A, P, D, L)
```

```
You searched for the AUTHOR: walker alice
19 entries found              LOCATIONS          CALL #
Walker Alice 1944
  1  The color purple:        Reserve Stack  PS3573.A425 C6
     a novel                  1982
  2  The dreaded comparison:  Book Stack     HV4708.S63 1988
     human and ani
  3  Five poems               Special Co     PS3573.A425 F5
  4  Good night, Willie Lee,  Special Co     PS3573.A425 G6
     I'll see you I
  5  Her blue body everything Book Stack     PS3573.A425 H47 1991
     we know: ear
  6  Horses make a landscape
     look more beau           Book Stack     PS3573.A425 H6 1984
  7  I love myself when I am   Book Stack     PS3513.U789 A56 1979
     laughing . . . a
  8  In love & trouble;       Book Stack     PS3573.A425 I5
     stories of Black wo
  9  In search of our         Reserve St     PS3573.A425 Z467 198
     mothers' gardens: wo
 10  Langston Hughes,         Juvenile S     PS3515.U274 Z9
     American poet.
 11  Meridian                 Book Stack     PS3573.A425 M4 1986
 12  Once; poems              Book Stack     PS3573.A425 O5
 13  Possessing the           Book Stack     PS3573.A425 P67 1992
     secret of joy
 14  Revolutionary petunias   Book Stack     PS3573.A425 R4
     & other poems
 15  The same river twice:    Book Stack
     honoring the di
 16  The temple of my familiar Book Stack    PS3573.A425 T46 1989
 17  To hell with dying       Juvenile S     P27.W15213 To 1988
 18  Warrior marks: female    Book Stack     GN484.W35 1993
     genital mutilat
 19  You can't keep a good    Book Stack     PS3573.A425 Y6
     woman down: sto




Please type the NUMBER of the item you want to see, OR
B > Go BACKWARD               A > ANOTHER Search by AUTHOR
R > RETURN to Browsing        P > PRINT
N > NEW Search                + > ADDITIONAL options
Choose one (1-19, B, R, N, A, P, L, J, E, U, +)
```

If more than one author is listed, choose the author that you would like to search by entering the code or number next to that author's name and an additional command. You will bring up another screen. There you will find a list of all of the books by that author that the library owns.

By entering the code found next to the book you would like to find, the next screen will give you information about the chosen book.

This screen will provide you with bibliographic information, the call number, location information that describes if the book is located in a special collection (such as Reference, Reserve, etc.), and whether or not the book is on the shelf.

```
                       Record 17 or 19
AUTHOR        Walker, Alice, 1944-
TITLE         To  hell  with  dying  /  by  Alice  Walker;
              illustrated by Catherine Deeter.
PUBL. INFO.   San Diego: Harcourt Brace Jovanovich,
              1988.
DESCRIPT      [32] p.:col. Ill.; 26 x 28 cm.
SUBJECT       Afro-Americans—Fiction.
              Friendship—Fiction.
NOTE          The  author  relates  how  old  Mr.  Sweet,
              though often on the verge of dying, could
              always be revived by the loving attention
              that she and her brother gave him.
ADDL AUTHOR   Deeter, Catherine.
LOCATION            CALL NO.          STATUS
1 > Juvenile Stacks   PZ7.W15213 To 1988   ON THE SHELF
```

**Title search.** This method enables you to search for a resource for which you know the title. When you do a title search, you will be asked to type the title of the book and then press an additional command key. The next screen will provide a list of titles. The title that you requested, or the closest match that the system can find to your request, will be highlighted. If there is no match, many systems will identify where your title would be in the list if it could be located. If your title is matched, you can bring up the next screen by entering the code number next to the title. That screen will provide you with identifying information, including author, call number, and date and place of publication.

**Subject search.** Use a subject search to locate resources about a particular topic area. This kind of search is most useful when you have identified a research area, but do not know any authors who write about the subject or titles of specific books. Most on-line catalogues offer two kinds of subject searches:

- **Key word/Title word search.** Allows you to search for a resource by entering words that describe your subject. The on-line catalogue will search all of the library's holdings that include your combination of words. When the search is complete, a screen will be displayed that contains a list of all of the sources that contain those words, or related terms, in the title.
- **Library of Congress Subject Headings.** Searches for resources that pertain to a subject classified by the Library of Congress. Check the bound volumes for the correct subject classification, then enter that heading. You will see a screen that lists all of the holdings that the library owns that are in that category. If you have difficulty conducting your search, be certain to check that you are using the correct term.

## Closing Thoughts

The library skills discussed in this chapter are among the most challenging that a college student has to learn. They are complex and difficult to master. It will take several months of continual practice before you are proficient and, even then, surprises are continually in store whenever you are doing library research. These skills will be invaluable, however, because the ability to gather information is the key to finding the facts and making good decisions, whether in business, in areas of personal interest, or in academic assignments. Nobody is going to take you by the hand and train you in how to use the library. It is a task you must take on yourself and constantly practice so you will have the skill when you need it. The practice will pay off, however, when the secrets of the library become yours to use.

## EXERCISE 18

# Narrowing and Broadening Topics

*Instructions:* *Select a topic and narrow it downward and broaden it upward as thoroughly as you can. For example, if you were given the topic of "Dogs," you would narrow it and broaden it using the sample provided. The purpose of this exercise is to demonstrate the process that researchers have to go through in determining the scope of their research. The broader the scope, the more information there is available and the more general it tends to be. The narrower the topic, the more specialized the information tends to be. Thus, if you want to write a large, general piece (such as a survey textbook or a general background article), you would select a broader topic. If you want to write a specialized, original piece (such as an article for a highly specialized journal or an original piece of scientific research), you would select a narrower topic. Choose a topic that is important to you. You may investigate career choices, explore information for a research paper in another class, or learn more about a social or political issue. If you are having trouble thinking of a topic, see the following list for ideas.*

### Sample Topic Narrowing and Broadening

Broader Topics:     Biological Life Forms
                    Vertebrate Animals
                    Mammals
                    Domesticated Animals
                    Household Pets

Original Topic:     Dogs

Narrower Topics:    Sheepdogs
                    English Sheepdogs
                    Raising English Sheepdogs
                    The Business of Breeding English Sheepdogs
                    Breeding English Sheepdogs in California
                    Profitability of Breeding English Sheepdogs in Los Angeles

List of possible topics:    Kenya              Horses
                            Amazon River       Advertising
                            Paintings          Basketball
                            Great Wall of China    Carrots
                            German Opera       Moby Dick

# Worksheet

**Broader Topics:** _____

_____

_____

_____

_____

_____

_____

_____

_____

**Original Topic:** _____

**Narrower Topics:** _____

_____

_____

_____

_____

_____

_____

_____

_____

_____

_____

_____

# Locating Library Resources

*Instructions: Arrange a tour of your campus library or explore on your own to locate the following resources which your library holds. Write specific instructions on their location so that a stranger to your library could find them easily.*

1. *Library of Congress Subject Headings:*

2. On-line Catalogue:

3. Specialized Computer Databases:

4. Reference Room:

5. General Encyclopedias:

6. *Reader's Guide to Periodical Literature:*

7. Reserve Room:

8. Periodical Room (or where the bound periodicals are located):

9. *Books in Print:*

10. Special Services (specify and locate one):

# Using the Resources of the Library

*Instructions: Select a topic from among the list of topics you developed in Exercise 18 and locate in the library a resource in each of the following categories that gives you information about this topic. When recording the book or article you find, use a complete bibliographic citation that includes the following elements:*

Sample citations:

- Article in an encyclopedia:

  "Dogs," *Encyclopedia Britannica,* Vol. 26, 1985, pp. 415–423.
- Book:

  John Author, *The Big Book of Dogs* (New York: Prospect Books, 1996).
- Magazine article:

  Mary Author, "Raising Your Sheepdog," *Pet Owner's Magazine* 45 (September 1996), pp. 78–80.

## Framing the Research Question

Before you begin your research, determine your purpose. You may have selected a topic area, but what exactly do you want to know about that topic? (You may use your topic from Exercise 18, an assignment from another class, or you may investigate career opportunities for your major.) The clearer your purpose, the easier it is to determine whether a book or magazine will give you the information you need. Determine a specific purpose for conducting research on your chosen topic. Keep this purpose in mind as you then try to find resources that will give you information. If you have trouble with this step, check with your instructor for advice before beginning.

Topic Area: _____

Specific Research Goal: _____

_____

_____

_____

_____

_____

_____

_____

## 1. Library of Congress Subject Headings

Look for your topic (or related key words) in this resource. Is it listed as a major heading (in bold type)? What are some of the related headings or sub-headings listed with it: RT (Related Term), BT (Broader Term), or NT (Narrower Term)? If your topic word is not listed, what related words are listed that would help you find information on your topic?

Topic Heading:  _____

Related Headings:

## 2. General Encyclopedias

To find information about your topic (or an alternative heading) in a general encyclopedia, search for the topic word in the encyclopedia index first (usually a separate volume at the end of the encyclopedia). List below the topic heading you used, the names of the various articles in which your topic is discussed, and the complete citation for one article.

Topic Heading:  _____

Articles in which the topic is discussed (from the encyclopedia index):

One specific article citation:

### 3. Subject Dictionaries and Special Encyclopedias

Subject dictionaries and encyclopedias provide more specialized information than general encyclopedias. Locate these resources by looking under the "Subject" entry in a computer catalogue under your topic heading. For example, if you are researching dogs, the subject heading to look for is: "Dogs—Dictionaries and Encyclopedias." If your topic word is not listed, try a broader related heading. For example, if there were no subject heading dictionaries for "Dogs," look under the entry "Pets—Dictionaries and Encyclopedias." List below the citation for the article you found on your topic.

Topic Heading: _____

Article Citation:

### 4. On-Line Title Search

Conduct a title search for any books whose titles begin with your topic word. List the library call number and give the complete citation (author, title, city, publisher, date) for **two** books (if there are any listed). Note: Using a title search for general research is not very effective because only a few of the books available on your topic will begin their titles with the topic word. Once you find the citations for books in other sources, such as in the footnotes or bibliographies of other books or magazine articles, a title search will be more useful.

Topic Heading: _____

Call
Number:

Complete
Citation:

Call
Number:

Complete
Citation:

### 5. On-Line Author Search

Conduct an author search for any books on your topic written by an author whose works you already know. List the library call number and give the complete citation for two books (if there are any listed). Note: Using an author search for general research is not very effective because only a few of the books available on your topic will be written by a writer with whom you are familiar. Once you are further along investigating your topic, you will learn the names of the leading authors in that field and an author search will be more useful.

Topic Heading: _____

Call
Number:                                    Complete
                                           Citation:

Call
Number:                                    Complete
                                           Citation:

### 6. On-Line Key Word Search

Conduct a key word search for books that deal with your topic. List below the topic word that you looked for and **two** books that you think would be useful in your research. Include the library call number and the complete citation. Locate the books on the library shelves and briefly skim them.

Topic word(s) _____

Call
Number:                                    Complete
                                           Citation:

Call
Number:                                    Complete
                                           Citation:

Did you notice any related books nearby on the shelf that could be useful? List the call number and citation for one book that you found on the shelf by browsing.

Call
Number:                                    Complete
                                           Citation:

## 7. Library of Congress Subject Heading Search

Conduct a search for books that deal with your topic by using a subject heading from the *Library of Congress Subject Headings*. List below the subject heading that you looked for and **two** books that you think would be useful in your research. Include the library call number and the complete citation. If you cannot locate any books, recheck the subject heading in the bound volumes of *Library of Congress Subject Headings*.

Subject Heading: _____

Call
Number:

Complete
Citation:

Call
Number:

Complete
Citation:

## 8. Reserve Materials Search

Follow the directions in the on-line catalogue to conduct a search of materials on Reserve. Enter the name of one of your instructors or the title of one of your courses to see if any materials are being held in the Reserve Room for use by that instructor in that class. List the materials on Reserve.

Instructor:

Department:

Course title and number:

Complete citation for one reserve item:

Loan period:

# Expanding a Topic Search

*Instructions: Using the topic that you developed for Exercise 18 and that you researched for Exercise 20, expand your research to include periodicals, specialized databases, and other libraries.*

Topic: _____

## 1. On-Line Periodical Search

Use one of the on-line periodical search programs (e.g., National Newspaper Search, InfoTrack, Lexus/Nexus) to investigate your topic. Limit your search to the last five years. Provide complete citations for three or four articles.

Name of Search Program: _____

Title of article:

Author of article:

Periodical:

Volume, number, date:

Pages:


Title of article:

Author of article:

Periodical:

Volume, number, date:

Pages:


Title of article:

Author of article:

Periodical:

Volume, number, date:

Pages:


## 2. Reader's Guide to Periodical Literature

This index is a guide to popular magazine articles. Look in the guide for two articles on your topic. List the citations for these articles below. Check the library's list of periodicals (a catalogue of all the periodicals and magazines stored in your library) to see if the library subscribes to the periodical or magazine you want. Individual magazines are often given library call numbers so that you can locate them on the shelves yourself. Write the call numbers of the two citations you found. Go to the Periodical Room and locate the periodicals or magazines that contain the articles you want to read.

Topic Heading: _____

Call number:

Title of article:

Author of article:

Periodical:

Volume, number, date:

Pages:


Call number:

Title of article:

Author of article:

Periodical:

Volume, number, date:

Pages:


### 3. Specialized Database Search

Identify a specialized database that would include your topic. There are many such databases that catalogue resources in education, psychology, business, arts, and other subjects. Locate two new sources (book or periodicals) in a specialized database and provide complete citations for each resource.

Database: _____

Citation for Source #1:          Citation for Source #2:


### 4. Searching Another Library

Access the on-line catalogue, and choose to view the holdings of another library. Conduct a key word search to see if you can find one book that is available at another library but not at your school's library. Provide the complete citation.

Name of library searched: _____

Call
Number:

Complete
Citation:

# 6

## "Why does communicating have to be so hard?"

Most students hate to write. And even worse than writing is the thought of giving a speech. These two communication skills, however, are among the most valued in academic and professional life. More than any other skill, the ability to express yourself clearly and confidently in writing or in public speaking marks you as a competent and intelligent person.

Despite the importance attached to these skills, however, few students enjoy writing or speaking. They often sit staring at a blank page, stumped by writer's block when they have to compose an essay or write a report. Often they are petrified by stage fright when they have to give an oral report or make a speech in a class. If these skills are so important, why do students hate them so?

The answer to this question lies in *avoidance*. People develop skill in an activity by practicing. The more skill people have in an activity, the more they tend to enjoy it. If they avoid practicing an activity, they never develop skill, and thus they never learn to enjoy it. The vicious circle of avoidance, lack of practice, lack of enjoyment, and avoidance keeps people unskilled and unhappy. This is why students hate writing and speaking so much. Typically, they have had unpleasant experiences with writing or speaking and consequently avoid it as much as possible. This avoidance leads to maintaining the poor skills that prevent them from ever being motivated to improve.

How does one break this vicious circle of avoidance? Sometimes, an effective instructor or a coach can provide a positive environment that makes it easier for students to overcome their initial resistance to practicing communication skills. An effective instructor gives positive feedback to encourage students to practice and develop skills so they can improve. If you have been fortunate, you have had instructors who helped you to develop writing and speaking skills and to learn to enjoy expressing yourself.

Unfortunately, though, many students have never become excited and motivated about communication skills. If they want to break out of this vicious circle, they must motivate themselves to do it. This is a much harder goal, but it is possible. If you know that your writing and speaking skills are not as fully developed and enjoyable as you would like, you can improve them. All it takes is practice. But you must motivate yourself to stick to the task of improving.

This chapter suggests some techniques for improving your writing and speaking skills as they relate to the college classroom:

- analyzing an assignment;
- basic writing skills;
- basic public speaking skills.

These suggestions will help you improve and enjoy writing and speaking assignments. The first step is yours, however. You must make a firm commitment to work at the exercises that will improve these skills, or improvement will never come. Learning to write or to speak is hard work, but so is playing basketball, shopping, or cooking gourmet meals. The difference is that people spend time practicing and developing skills in the latter areas without ever thinking about the pain. Writing and speaking can be just as enjoyable as any other activity once you have developed skill and start getting positive reinforcement for your accomplishments in these areas. The exercises at the end of this chapter will help you to develop these skills.

# Analyzing an Assignment

Have you ever put in many hours doing research and writing only to turn in the paper and hear the instructor say, "This was not exactly what I was looking for"? Or have you ever gone to the library and worked hard on an assignment, but ended up staring at the wall for hours because you kept thinking, "I don't know exactly what I'm trying to do." If you have ever found yourself in these situations, you need to address the challenge of analyzing an assignment.

In terms of writing and speaking for college assignments, you are not working in a vacuum. An instructor usually gives guidelines about what to say (content), how to say it (style), and what form to put it in (format). The key to making assignments easier and more successful is to get clear instructions before you begin. A clear purpose and writing plan will save you much time and energy. The following suggestions will help to clarify your purpose and give you a headstart on research and writing effectively.

1. **Understand what the instructor wants.** When they give assignments, instructors are not always perfectly clear. Cynical students might say that such instructors are playing a sort of guessing game in which students have to figure out the assignment for themselves. More commonly, instructors are not trying to be difficult, but because of time pressures or oversight they do not provide adequate explanations of their goals and criteria for an assignment. Any of these drawbacks can be overcome, fortunately, by talking to the instructor individually about your understanding of the assignment in terms of content, style, and format. Ask questions, either as the instructor makes the assignment in class or individually during the instructor's office hours. Ask for the specific details of what the instructor wants in the content, style, and format for the assignment. It is also useful to ask how the assignment will be evaluated.

2. **Discuss assignments with the instructor.** If you are unclear about an assignment, the first thing you should do is talk to the instructor about it. You might consult with fellow students to see if they understand it, but chances are that if you are confused, other students are likely to be confused, too. Don't trust their misconceptions. Go straight to the source and talk to the instructor yourself. The instructor will notice your extra effort and will probably be willing to give you extra time and attention. Ask questions about the scope of the assignment, which topics might work better than others, how to broaden or narrow the topic appropriately, where you can possibly find information, and anything that you should take care to avoid.

3. **First try to figure out the assignment on your own.** When you go to talk with an instructor, do not expect him to do your thinking for you. Struggle with the assignment and generate

a few ideas that you want to weigh with the instructor's advice. It is far better to have several ideas of your own and then to ask for the instructor's suggestions for improvement than to walk in totally in the dark because you have not even thought about the assignment.

4. **Determine the larger purpose of an assignment.** Most college assignments fit into some big picture that an instructor has for the course. Work to understand how assignments logically build upon each other and how they fit into the overall scope of the entire course. By understanding this larger purpose for an assignment, you will more likely see what the instructor is trying to accomplish by having you do it.

5. **Understand the criteria by which assignments will be graded.** Instructors usually have a clear picture of what they want in an assignment. You have to get them to tell you the "right way" and the "wrong way" of getting it done. Ask for the specific standards by which the instructor will evaluate the assignment. Ask for common problems with the assignment the instructor has seen in the past and pitfalls to avoid. If possible, get a sample of an outstanding assignment so you can see for yourself what the instructor is talking about. Good instructors include these points in their explanation of an assignment, but you may have to remind them by asking.

6. **Determine the difference between good and bad content, style, and format.** Discuss with your instructor these three elements of the assignment:

- **content:** what ideas to include or exclude, the broadness or narrowness of scope for the assignment, which sources to use in doing research, the kinds of information the instructor wants in the assignment, what makes for good and bad information to include in the assignment;

- **style:** the kind of language that will be most appropriate in writing your assignment, the level of formality or informality the instructor wants, the use of jargon or terminology that is most appropriate;

- **format:** how the instructor wants the assignment to look physically—typing, spacing, layout of the pages, use of a title page, bindings, footnotes, bibliography, and other elements such as pictures, appendices, or graphs.

Fifteen minutes spent on these concerns at the beginning of a project can save you hours of wasted effort and frustration later on. In addition, when you discuss the project with your instructors, they can give you some ideas to include or things to consider that you would never have thought of on your own.

7. **Start early and plan to finish early.** The best way to perform well on assignments is to show your instructor that you are

working hard. By talking to your instructor early about an assignment (immediately after it is given is the best time), you demonstrate that you are planning ahead and thinking about excellence. By finishing the project early, you give your instructor the chance to review your first draft and make suggestions for improvements. Many instructors are willing to give you the chance to improve the project even further before you turn it in for a grade.

## Basic Writing Skills

Do you know how to walk? What a silly question, right? Of course you know how to walk—you do it all the time without thinking about it. But consider for a moment all the different types of walking: across the room, down to the corner market, a 10-mile hike through the forest, an expedition up the Matterhorn, or speed walking in the Olympics. Each one is walking, but each is remarkably different from the other forms and requires quite different modes of training and practice in order to do it successfully.

The simple walking we do each day—across the room or down to the market—lulls us into a false sense of understanding what walking is. If you were to attempt a climb up the Matterhorn—or even a 10-mile hike through the woods on a hot day—with the same level of preparation as everyday walking, you might be in for some rude, even dangerous, awakenings. You need to be much more expert to hike long distances, climb mountains, or compete in the Olympics if you are going to do those activities safely and successfully.

The same is true of writing. We often assume that we know what is involved because we all do simple writing every day. But college will require a level of writing that is more professional and scholarly than any that you have probably experienced before. Unless you learn these methods of writing and practice them at this new professional level, you will be like the average person setting off unprepared for the Matterhorn. Trouble, even disaster, awaits!

The following suggestions will help you write more professionally. If you have had good writing training, many of them may be familiar to you. Most students, however, say that writing is one of the most difficult and least pleasant activities they do in college. By learning to write in a professional manner, you will make your writing much easier, much more satisfying, and much more highly evaluated.

1. **Before you write, clarify your purpose.** The key to analyzing an assignment, as discussed, is in understanding your purpose by figuring out what you want to say in light of what an instructor is looking for in the requirements of the assignment. The same step is necessary for writing, no matter what you are going to write. Use the techniques discussed above for clarifying your

purpose: talk to people about your project, understand the criteria by which your writing will be evaluated, get feedback from the person who will be evaluating your writing, look at samples if possible, start early, and try to finish the first draft early so you can have a chance to revise it.

2. **Before you write, organize your thoughts.** Use an outline to guide your thinking process. Several different types of outlines can help you:

- **tentative outline:** a preliminary planning outline that contains random ideas you might use. Good writers use "jot lists," "laundry lists," "brain maps" of random ideas, or just key words to help get their ideas initially organized.

- **working outline:** a rough first draft of the outline that will guide you as your write. This outline should always be tentative, because in the middle of writing you may come up with good ideas that you want to include. As these new ideas come to you, always go back and change your working outline so you can remember them and stay organized.

- **test outline:** a tool for analyzing first drafts. Once you have completed the first draft of a piece of writing, it is a good idea to compose an outline of what you actually have on paper and analyze it. Look for balance between the items, completeness of the ideas, and logical order of the parts. If there are flaws in any of these areas, the test outline will help you plan the second draft and incorporate these improvements.

- **final outline:** a formal outline of a completed document. Once you have gone through all your preliminary drafts and have a final draft of a paper, you can complete the final outline. Most people make the mistake of starting with the final outline first and not using the other forms. Good writing emerges through several drafts and several outlines.

3. **Use a three-part structure to write.** All good writing relies upon three parts to accomplish certain functions. Your purpose and format often determine what is included in each part, but these general guidelines apply:

- **introduction:** the purpose of the introduction is to prepare the reader for what will follow in the document. Usually the writer wants to grab the reader's attention, create a sense of need or concern about the topic, establish some credibility, announce the topic of the document, and sometimes even give a pre-summary of the main points of the body.

- **body:** the largest part of a document is the body, which presents the main points of information. The main points should be clearly organized and supported with facts or evidence. Under each main point in the body, supporting ideas reinforce and explain the main ideas.

- **conclusion:** a document can end in many different ways. The writer can summarize by repeating the main points of the body, draw conclusions about what has been presented in the body, suggest or recommend future action, or leave the reader with a final, interesting thought about the topic.

4. **Use paragraphs to organize the document.** Paragraphs organize your ideas logically and help the reader see the structure of the ideas on the written page. Use separate paragraphs for each distinct idea in the document. Good paragraphs consist of an introductory **thesis sentence,** which announces what the paragraph will discuss, and **supporting sentences,** which provide more details, examples, or explanations about the thesis of the paragraph.

5. **Use transitions to link your ideas.** A transition is a word or a phrase or even an entire sentence announcing to the reader that you are moving from one idea to another. Transitions can also explain how your ideas are interconnected, thus demonstrating your organizational structure. Writing that is clearly structured is easier to read and understand than writing that seems to ramble. Use transitional words and phrases to perform the following functions:

---

*Sample Transitions*

| *Transitional Function* | *Example (Key Words)* |
| --- | --- |
| Emphasis | first, most important, mainly |
| Enumeration | first, second, next, then, last |
| Comparison | similarly, likewise, in the same vein |
| Contrast | on the other hand, in contrast |
| Addition | moreover, in addition, another point |
| Provide example | for example, to prove my point |
| Relationship | related, supporting, connected |
| Conclusion | in summary, finally, to conclude, thus |

---

6. **Be complete.** As you plan and write, keep in mind how much you need to say to satisfy the reader's needs. Do you want a superficial surface coverage, or do you want to go into elaborate detail? It is often difficult to draw the line between too little and too much information, but it is necessary to determine this factor to know what level of detail will be appropriate for the reader. If you are writing for an instructor, analyze the guidelines or discuss them so you include everything you should in your writing. Once you have completed the writing, compare it to the guidelines to make sure you have not omitted anything important. If you are unclear about what to include or omit, discuss these concerns in advance with your instructor.

7. **Be accurate.** Correct grammar, punctuation, and spelling are essential elements of good writing. If you have questions about correct usage as you write, consult a writer's handbook or a dictionary. If you have serious problems in these areas, consider additional work in English composition and writing to build up your skills.

8. **Use a second draft to perfect your writing style.** Few writers can write well in a first draft. Good writing comes from rewriting. If you want to excel as a writer, plan to edit your first draft, correct any errors, rework any awkward sentences, and reorganize if necessary. Plan your time so you can write a second, or even a third, draft. The only way to learn to write is by rewriting. To prove the point, read something you wrote several months ago. Now that you have had time to think about it, wouldn't you do better on a second draft?

9. **Proofread.** Once you have completed the final draft of a document, carefully proofread for any mistakes that may have crept into it. If possible, have another person proofread your work. It is easier to be objective and to catch errors in someone else's writing. It is difficult to proofread your own writing, because you know what it is supposed to say and your eye may not catch a typographical error.

## Basic Public Speaking Skills

Only a few students (usually theater or speech majors) relish the thought of giving a speech in front of others. The ability to speak effectively and confidently in public, however, is a valuable skill that will serve you well throughout your life. College offers many opportunities to practice this skill: oral reports, in-class recitation, debates, discussions, and formal speeches. Skill and comfort in public speaking come only from practice, so the more you practice public speaking, the better you will become at this skill.

Many colleges require a public speaking class because it is such an important skill. Do not wait until speech class, however, to begin developing your speech-making skills. Every time you have to talk in public, you can take one more step on the road to becoming a better speaker if you concentrate on organizing and practicing your speaking skills. The following guidelines should help in planning your next public speech.

1. **Analyze your audience.** Consider the interests and values of the members of the audience so your remarks will be relevant and useful to them. Do not waste their time by talking about things that are of no value to them. If you cannot think of interesting or valuable things to say, discuss the topic with your instructor or people you know in the audience to get ideas as you plan the speech.

2. **Plan your thoughts by outlining your speech.** Writing a speech is similar to writing an essay. Planning is important for getting organized. To prevent rambling and getting lost, organize your thoughts in an outline. As with good writing, a good speech consists of an introduction, the main points (the body of the speech), and a conclusion.

3. **Concentrate on what you have to say, not on your performance.** As you plan the speech, keep foremost in your mind the information you have to present. If you have something valuable and worthwhile to say, people will not care what you look like or how you present the information. This attitude will prevent you from building up a great deal of stage fright.

4. **Begin by grabbing attention and clarifying your purpose.** An effective introduction should whet the audience members' appetite for the rest of the speech. Begin with an attention-grabbing idea. Then explain how your remarks will be relevant and useful to the audience. Provide some information about yourself so the audience will know you a little better. Announce the topic clearly and summarize the main points of the body in advance.

5. **Support your main ideas with facts and interest features.** For each main point, provide relevant facts and examples. This information usually comes from adequate research. Make the main points interesting by including personal experiences, interesting stories that support the point you are making, experiences that the audience has had related to your topic, or visual aids such as pictures, objects, charts, or graphs.

6. **End with a strong conclusion.** A good speech should be ended by a summary of the points covered in the body, a conclusion that pulls the main points together into a final thought, and a strong last line that leaves a positive impression of the speaker.

7. **Control nervousness by preparing thoroughly.** Every speaker has stage fright to some degree. The only way to control your nerves is to plan carefully and rehearse. The more you rehearse, the more confident you will feel. Rehearse the speech aloud and in front of a practice audience. Get feedback about how the speech might be improved and practice it again.

8. **Control your physical delivery by relaxing.** Try to relax in front of the audience. Smile, take deep breaths, and take your time. Members of the audience want you to succeed; they are on your side. If you make a mistake, simply correct it and continue. Do not draw attention to it by apologizing. Try to look at the audience members and be certain they understand what you are saying.

9. **Try to enjoy yourself.** Public speaking is somewhat like acting. Even if you are nervous, you should act like you are confident and relaxed. By looking relaxed, you will help audience members to relax and enjoy your presentation. They will focus on your content and not on your delivery.

## Closing Thoughts

As the earlier analogy stated, writing is like walking. Most people can walk, but not everyone is ready to climb the Matterhorn. Excellence in most careers requires excellent communication skills, so you may want to start a training program to prepare you for the professional mountains you will be facing in your future.

Effective communication is hard work, but it underlies all of your college career. If you can develop the skills of writing and speaking, you will gain a valuable career asset that will pay dividends throughout the rest of your life. Improving communications skill takes concerted effort. You have to break many ingrained habits by learning and practicing new behaviors. One class in English composition or public speaking is usually not enough to change years of bad habits. Be honest about your skill level, and commit yourself to improving in this vital area if you need to improve.

# Analyzing an Assignment

*Instructions: Use the following worksheet to discuss and plan for an upcoming assignment with an instructor in another class.*

*1. Before you visit the instructor, explain the assignment as you understand it.*

*2. Prepare a set of questions (based on the suggestions in this chapter) to ask your instructor that will help you understand the assignment more fully. (You may need additional sheets of paper.) In the space after each question, keep notes of your instructor's answers and the discussion.*

*3. Finally, comment on the value of conducting this interview.*

1. What is the purpose and scope of the assignment as you now understand it?

2. Questions for the instructor:                    Notes on answers:




3. Comments on the value of this exercise:

# Writing an Essay

*Instructions:*

*Step 1. In 30 minutes, plan and write an essay on the topic "Why the library is such a valuable resource for college students." Pay attention to your writing skills and demonstrate your knowledge of the resources in the library. Plan and outline your answer on this page, and add extra blank pages for the text of your essay.*

*Step 2. Once you have completed your answer, critique it with a partner, comparing your answer to your partner's. Look again at the suggestions in this chapter. Look at the following questions to see how your answer might be improved.*

Essay topic:   Why the Library is Such a Valuable Resource
                 for College Students

Preliminary Outline:

Here's a checklist for improving the essay. Use the extra space for notes about improving the essay.

☐ Does your essay start with a strong, positive statement and preview the main points you will make in the body of the essay?

☐ Is your essay organized into an introductory paragraph, separate paragraphs for each of the main points (or reasons), and a concluding paragraph?

☐ Does each paragraph begin with a clear thesis sentence that states what the paragraph will cover?

☐ Is each paragraph supported by facts, examples, and explanations relevant to the thesis of that paragraph?

☐ Does the essay conclude with a paragraph that reasserts the opening statement and gives a sense of closure to the essay?

☐ Did you proofread the essay once you completed it?

☐ How accurate is the essay in terms of spelling, punctuation, and grammar?

# Giving a Public Speech

*Instructions:* *Attend a meeting of a student organization on your campus. Names of clubs and announcements of their meetings are available in the student newspaper, on posters across campus, and from the office of student activities.*

*Prepare a five-minute speech to deliver to your class that reports your impressions of the organization you visited. Your speech should cover the following topics:*

- *the name of the organization you visited;*
- *the services or activities that this organization provides;*
- *what happened at the meeting you attended;*
- *your final impressions of the value of this organization to students.*

*Follow the guidelines in this chapter on organizing and presenting a speech. Use the following worksheet to plan your speech. (Feel free to add extra items to the ones suggested in this outline.)*

Speech Title:

Presenter:

I. Introduction
A. Attention grabbing opening line:

B. Why this speech will be important or useful:

C. Topic of your speech:

D. Preview of the main points:

II. Body
A. Overview of the organization's activities and services:
1.

2.

3.

B. What happened at the meeting you attended:
1.

2.

3.

C. Your impressions of the value of the organization:
1.

2.

3.

III. Conclusion
A. Your final assessment of this organization:

B. Whether you would recommend that other students join it:

C. Strong last line to end the speech:

# 7

## "Did we do anything important last class?"

One of the sad truths of college life that you will learn, if you have not already, is that instructors vary in quality. Some are good, and some are not so good! As expert observers of instructors (you have at least 12 years of observation already), you have probably seen different kinds of instructors at work, and you know firsthand the effects their techniques have on students. In college you will encounter the same thing: some excellent instructors and some whose courses will be less than enjoyable. In fact, ineffective instructors in college become an impediment to their students and can actually make learning more difficult.

The effect that poor teaching can have on students is clear. In the long run, a poor instructor undermines the motivation of students and destroys any interest they might have in the subject matter. Students do not attend classes that are uninteresting, and they do not apply themselves to study such classes. As a result, students are not introduced to possible career opportunities and skills that would benefit them in the future. In the short run, it becomes difficult for students to get high grades in courses for which they care little about the subject and are not motivated to study.

Fortunately, most college instructors are professional. They take their jobs seriously and provide a quality education to students who are paying, and often making great sacrifices, to attend school. Unfortunately, you may occasionally encounter less than the ideal, so you must learn how to cope with any inferior instructors you may run across. By taking responsibility for your own education, you can get quality instruction in spite of any poor teaching techniques you might encounter. This chapter will introduce you to the idea of teaching style and suggest methods you can use to get the most out of your instructors, whatever their methods. Finally, the chapter will address the issue of grades and suggest techniques you can use in any class to improve your grades.

## What Is Instructor Style?

From your years of observing instructors, you probably have concrete ideas of what makes for a good instructor. In polling students, the same description of a good instructor consistently emerges: someone who likes students, is enthusiastic about the subject matter, is well organized, is an interesting speaker, and is a fair grader. Do these sound like what you want in a instructor? The way a instructor behaves in these five categories—personal attitudes toward students, attitudes toward the subject matter, organizational skills, communication skills, and grading practices—is what constitutes **instructor style.** Instructors have many different styles; thus, the great variety in how instructors perform their jobs. By looking at the specific techniques in the chart below, you can gain a better idea of the challenge confronting instructors who want to be excellent. You might also gain some insight in how to help poor instructors become better if you offer them feedback on course evaluations.

Many more characteristics probably fall under these five categories, and each behavior can be performed in many different ways. For example, the single item about "provides review sessions" as a grading practice might be done with handout review sheets, an in-class review session before the exam, a separate review session at night, a take-home practice exam, or a review session exercise in which students conduct the review. Thus, a instructor can develop her style in many different ways.

*Attributes of Excellent Instructors*

- **Positive attitude toward students:** Is willing to interact with students individually, knows students' names, calls students by name, is friendly and cheerful, is positive and optimistic about students' success in a class, is helpful and willing to give extra effort to help students succeed, respects students' problems and concerns, is willing to listen.

- **Positive attitude toward the subject:** Is knowledgeable in the topic, is able to answer questions clearly, sees the practical applications and value of a subject, is enthusiastic and excited about the subject, has experience beyond just the classroom, gives extra effort to make the subject interesting and relevant.

- **Organizational skills:** Keeps good records, shows up to class and office hours on time, prepares class materials in advance, schedules class time and assignments efficiently, has a clear grasp of the whole class, sees how the parts of a class fit together, gives clearly organized lectures and instructions on assignments, turns assignments back on time.

- **Communication skills:** Has good listening skills, has good problem-solving and counseling skills when students have problems, is comfortable and relaxed as a lecturer, gives good examples and illustrations, tells good stories that relate to the subject, uses visual aids in lectures to help students learn, leads good discussions, is approachable as a person.

- **Grading practices:** States clear expectations at the beginning of the class, has reasonable expectations for grades assigned, has good test-making skills, provides review sessions, seeks student reactions to testing practices, is willing to listen to students who disagree about grading, treats students equally when assigning grades.

As a student, you should be familiar with the many teaching methods so you can make suggestions to instructors about how they might improve a class. You can also employ many of these techniques on your own, even if the instructor does not require or include them in a course. For example, if a instructor does not hold review sessions for an exam, you might set up your own on an evening before the exam and invite several classmates to attend. When instructors see this sort of initiative in a student, they often recognize the value in the activity and begin to incorporate it into their styles. Thus, instead of complaining about poor instructors, you can actually affect their teaching methods by taking the initiative for getting a quality education—either by suggesting teaching techniques that you think would be helpful or by using the technique in your own "student style." Exercise 25 at the end of this chapter asks you to observe the teaching style of one of your instructors in order to develop your analytical and observation skills of instructors' styles and the methods they use.

While it is good for students to expect instructors to be understanding, it is also probably appropriate that instructors might expect the same from students. Many college instructors have never had any training in teaching methods. College instructors are hired because of their technical expertise in a subject matter. They are expected to develop their teaching methods on the job. Needless to say, this is a poor way to ensure quality teaching, so students should be on the lookout for inexperienced instructors and expect that they will need some extra understanding and guidance. College instructors also have many professional pressures on them besides teaching. Often their research publications, writing, and professional committee work count more toward their promotion and tenure than do their teaching evaluations. Being a good classroom instructor may rank low in their priorities, and they may need to be reminded of its importance to students.

All in all, being a good instructor is a difficult job. From the list of attributes above, you see how many types of skills and attitudes are required to be an excellent instructor. Everybody has good days and bad days, and instructors are human like anyone else. Thus you have to be patient with them. In order to get the most from your education, however, you need to know what you want from an instructor and how to make sure you get it. The following sections provide specific techniques for getting the most from good instructors and protecting yourself from the ones with whom you do not work effectively.

## How to Get the Most from Good Instructors

Being in the class of an excellent instructor is like watching a professional basketball player. Everything looks so simple and natural that you are not even aware of the vast skill being employed. It takes a lot of talent and years of hard practice to make the job look so easy. It is tempting to just sit back and "roll with the flow" and let the instructor run the whole show. You are missing a great opportunity, however. When you watch a basketball player, you are just a passive observer; with a good instructor, however, you are a part of the team. The activity cannot happen unless you are a part of it. When you are lucky enough to get a good instructor, you can do things to get even more out of the class than you ever thought possible. The following suggestions will help you get more from good instructors and turn a good class into one that could actually change the course of your college career.

1. **Get to know your instructors.** Probably the greatest single advantage of a good instructor is approachability—so approach! If you want an instructor to give you personal attention, you have to ask for it. Rarely will the instructor seek you out for an extended conversation. You must take the initiative to visit with the instructor, preferably during his office hours, and use the instructor to gather information that will be of use to you in your college and professional career. Good instructors are usually willing to talk about more than just the content of the class, though that is important to discuss, too. They are useful advisers concerning which classes to take, which instructors to avoid, career possibilities, where to find information for research projects you are working on, professional contacts once you start looking for a job, placement references, and all sorts of other college issues. An added advantage of knowing your instructor is that she will get to know you and will take an active interest in your career. If you are just another name on the roster or another face in a crowded classroom, you are missing one of the greatest educational resources your school has to offer. Even if it takes a few minutes before or after class, developing a working relationship with your instructors will pay off.

2. **Demonstrate your positive attitude about the class.** Just as you want instructors who have a positive attitude toward the subject matter, instructors want students to show interest and enthusiasm for a subject, too. You can demonstrate this attitude in your nonverbal signals as well as your comments about the class. Come to class early and get yourself organized to listen and take notes. Get involved by asking intelligent questions based on your reading of the assignment the night before. Smile and try to create a positive atmosphere in the classroom by volunteering and being helpful with other students. Your instructor will notice this behavior and appreciate it greatly.

3. **Demonstrate your respect for the instructor.** More than anything else, instructors want respect from students for themselves and for the subject matter of the class. How can you demonstrate this attitude? Respect for someone is usually expressed indirectly in the way in which you say things. There are "intelligent" questions and comments and there are "stupid" ones. Intelligent questions reveal underlying attitudes of respect:

- you have done some thinking prior to asking the question, not just putting all the responsibility for planning and thinking on the instructor;
- you are exerting effort in the class, not just expecting the instructor to do all the work and make things easy for you;
- you think the subject matter is valuable, not just a required headache you have to endure;

- you are willing to think the instructor will be helpful, not that he is out to make your life miserable by requiring boring homework;

- you are considerate of the instructor's feelings and status in the way you say things, not that you are concerned only about your own needs.

All instructors have pet peeves that irritate them because they are symptoms of a lack of respect. If you listen in on any group of teachers discussing students, they have similar complaints. The comments they hate to hear from students are listed below. Avoid making them. You can get the same information by just rephrasing the question in a more positive and respectful form, as suggested.

| *Things Instructors Hate to Hear* | *(Improved Version)* |
|---|---|
| "Why do I have to take this class?" | "Could you explain the reasons behind this course being required?" |
| "Do I have to do this assignment?" | "Will this assignment be required of everyone in the class?" |
| "Did we do anything important last time?" | "I'm sorry I missed class. I am concerned about the material I missed. What can I do?" |
| "I can't be here tomorrow—I've got something important to do." | "Would you please excuse me from class tomorrow? I have an important meeting. I will be glad to turn the assignment in early." |
| "You were not very clear about this last assignment." | "I am sorry, but I still do not understand this assignment. Could you explain it again?" |
| "I didn't hear you say that!" | "I am sorry. I must not have heard you say that. What can I do to correct my error?" |

Even neutral questions such as "What is going to be on the test?" or "When is this assignment due?" can be taken as disrespectful depending on the tone of voice used in asking them. Carefully communicating a respectful attitude toward the instructor and the class will pay off for you because the instructor will become much more receptive to your suggestions and requests if he or she trusts your motives. The better the instructor knows you, the more this trust will emerge. The result is a pleasant and relaxed classroom atmosphere that is highly conducive to learning.

4. **Demonstrate your competence beyond the instructor's expectations.** Most instructors sincerely want their students to learn the course content and to feel some of the appreciation they have for the subject. The best way to gain your instructor's respect is to demonstrate that you are working hard to master the subject. Go beyond the basic requirements for the course by asking for additional readings or by volunteering to do an especially demanding course project. Prepare thoroughly for each class, and plan several intelligent, probing questions that demonstrate you have done the reading and are thinking about the subject. Of course, time demands are always a consideration for you in taking on extra work, but you can impress your instructors in even small ways that you are working hard at the course. They will respect that and likely reward you for it.

5. **Provide feedback on how you learn best.** Once you have established a trusting, respectful relationship with an instructor, you are free to begin offering suggestions and ideas you know will be taken seriously. If you have concerns about how the course is being taught, the amount or kind of work due in the course, deadline dates, or other issues, you can approach the instructor and negotiate the requirements more to your satisfaction. Instructors need to know when their methods are an obstacle rather than an aid to learning. Below are nine steps to successful negotiation with an instructor that can help in providing feedback on how you best learn. Use them when you talk to an instructor about changes you would like to suggest in a course.

Negotiation does not always work, because some obstacles cannot be overcome and some instructors have policies they will not bend, but it is extremely useful for many situations in which rules are flexible. Again, the more an instructor knows and trusts you, the more likely he will be willing to negotiate, compromise, and give you the benefit of the doubt in tough situations. Exercise 28 at the end of this chapter will give you practice in negotiating.

Negotiation is a complex communication skill. It will take much practice for you to become proficient at using this skill. The benefits of good negotiation skills are great, however, and this technique is one you will be able to use throughout your life in many areas. It is worth the effort to develop the skill of negotiation.

6. **See the class from the instructor's perspective.** If you are lucky enough to have a good instructor, you can learn much from the craftsmanship and technique this instructor uses. Watch closely and observe the teaching methods and interpersonal skills of this good instructor. How would you describe this instructor's style in the five categories discussed earlier? What specific methods does the instructor use to teach and build rapport with students?

---

*The Nine Steps in Negotiating with Instructors*

1. **Start positively** by saying something good about the class or the instructor to begin the conversation on the right foot.

2. **State the overarching goal** that you both agree on by making it clear that you want the same things from the class that the instructor wants from you (to learn the subject matter and to perform well on the assignments).

3. **Explain the obstacle to your success** by explaining how some problem is preventing you from achieving the goal in Step 2 and that you are concerned.

4. **State some alternative solutions** and demonstrate that you have been thinking about the problem and have considered several different ways to solve it, but you need the instructor's advice or help to make the best choice.

5. **Ask for the instructor's input and opinions** to see if the instructor has any ideas or would be willing to do anything to help you.

6. **Compromise** until you find some middle-ground solution that is satisfactory to both of you. Use the reciprocity formula of "I will do X if you will do Y" to show that you are willing to sacrifice in order to satisfy the instructor.

7. **Make a verbal commitment** to the solution agreed upon. Make a deal with the instructor that demonstrates your resolve to abide by the agreement (take care here not to agree to something that you will not or cannot actually do).

8. **Thank the instructor** for the help offered.

9. **Stick to your bargain** (or come back and renegotiate later).

---

Watching a skilled practitioner in any endeavor will sharpen your awareness and analytical abilities. You will find that many of the same skills your instructor uses can be applied in your future career and relationships. Exercise 25 at the end of this chapter gives you the opportunity to critically observe a good instructor and identify the methods this instructor uses. Exercise 27 asks you to analyze a class in which you are having a problem to make suggestions for improvements.

7. **Become an active participant in your learning.** All of the techniques for getting the most from a good instructor boil down to your taking control of your own education and not leaving it up to the instructor. By providing the motivation for wanting to learn, you free the instructor's time so she can relax, make the class enjoyable, and get on with the show. Good instructors are able to motivate students to want to learn and provide information in an interesting way. The more you provide your own motivation by get-

ting actively involved in the learning process, the more time the instructor has to concentrate on making the subject matter interesting. In addition, the instructor will be more comfortable and able to listen to your suggestions on how the class can be even more satisfactory to you. Interestingly enough, the more you take on the high-motivation profile discussed in Chapter 1, the better all your instructors will tend to be, because you will know how to compensate for any weaknesses in method they might have and you can make the class work for you, no matter how skilled the instructor. Fortunately, too, instructors learn from their students, and you will be helping both yourself and the instructor in the long run. Instructors and students should be partners in the process.

## How to Cope with Instructors Who Do Not Fit Your Style

Each instructor's style is different. The instructor's personality will determine such things as the content of a course, how the content is covered, methods used to teach, and interpersonal relations with students. Likewise, each student has a different style: preferred ways of learning, unique interests, and an interpersonal style of relating to instructors. Occasionally you may meet instructors whose styles clash with yours. They might be too authoritarian when you want a casual classroom atmosphere. They may be too casual when you want a structured atmosphere. They may be too lecture-oriented when you want a discussion class. Thus, to ensure that you get an instructor from whom you can learn effectively, you must be aware of these differences in style. The more flexible you are, the more you can adapt to an instructor's style. The more flexible an instructor is, the more he can adjust to feedback from students. Despite this effort, mismatches may occur, and you need to know how to cope.

You should take care not to label an instructor as a bad match too quickly. Your first responsibility should be to try to train the instructor, by means of suggestions and feedback, in how to be more effective in teaching you. Most instructors will respond to these suggestions if you have built a trusting and respectful relationship with them. If you have genuinely tried to build a relationship and failed, however, you know you have trouble on your hands. The following suggestions are designed to help you find a match that is best for you and to help you cope with the situation if a mismatch should happen.

1. **Avoid potential problems.** The best solution, of course, is to avoid the problem altogether by researching instructors and classes in advance and staying clear of the instructors who have a reputation for being difficult to work with. Talk to students who

have taken the class, but be careful of unwarranted bias in student criticism. Some students unfairly criticize instructors for weaknesses in their own student styles. Make sure that critics know why they think an instructor is ineffective. Talk to faculty members you know and trust. Look at student evaluations if they are published on your campus. Interview the instructor in question the term before you expect to take that class. As you see, it takes some time and effort to protect yourself, but the results will far outweigh the wasted time and grief you will have to endure if you get stuck in an unpleasant class.

2. **Observe the instructor closely in the first class session.** Use the first class meeting to evaluate the instructor's style. Watch for signals that will telegraph the instructor's openness and willingness to work with students. Talk with the instructor after the class to get a personal feel for what she will be like. If you sense warning signals, do not persist in a course that you suspect will not be pleasant. Have alternative classes in mind that you can enroll in, and do more research to find a instructor for this particular course with whom you are more compatible. Depending upon your school's drop policy, you may be able to sample the class until the time of the first exam to make your assessment. Do not add classes late unless you absolutely have to. Joining a class late limits your ability to make a good first impression and start ahead of the rest of the class. You are automatically behind.

3. **Talk to the instructor.** If you think that your learning is being affected by certain teaching practices, by all means go to the instructor first. Try to negotiate a solution that is acceptable to both of you. You can complain to higher authorities, but the first question they will ask you is, "Have you talked to the instructor about this?" This should always be your starting point for any problem in a class.

4. **Complain to the proper authorities.** If you are stuck in an unpleasant class and cannot drop it, and if you have done all the constructive things you can to build a relationship and offer feedback, but none of these is working, then complain. Everyone has a boss, so go to the instructor's boss (whether it be department chair, dean of the school, or president of the university) and explain the situation. Use your negotiation skills to explain objectively and unemotionally what the instructor is doing to obstruct your progress in the class, what you have tried to do to remedy this situation, and what you want the authority to do. You may not get any action, because most college instructors are autonomous in their classrooms and are not subject to reprimand for their teaching styles. But if enough students complain, the message will begin to be heard by the instructor and by his or her institution that there is a problem that should be addressed.

5. **Do not wait until the end of the course to provide feedback.** If you are concerned about an instructor's methods or style,

do not wait until the end of the course to offer your suggestions. By then it is usually too late to do you any good. Build a relationship with the instructor and offer your suggestions so you can improve the class for your own benefit. It is extremely unfair of you to "blow an instructor out of the water" by giving a critical end-of-term evaluation if you have never tried to work with the instructor during the course.

6. **If you are forced to drop a course, let the instructor know why.** If you have done everything possible and have decided there is no way in which you can work with an instructor and must drop the course, let the instructor know exactly why you are leaving. In a personal interview (not in front of other students, please!), in a dispassionate and objective way, explain what you wanted and tried to get in the course and what the instructor did that was such an obstacle to your success. By this point (assuming you have tried to work with the instructor), you do not need to listen to excuses, nor should you take any abuse from the instructor. Just make your speech and leave. Of course, you should plan never to have to work with this instructor again, because you have jeopardized any possible positive relationship for the future, but if enough students give this instructor the same message, maybe the message will get through.

The cumulative effect of these unpleasant, but necessary, techniques for coping with instructors is that you begin to take responsibility for your own education. If an instructor is in the way of your learning or doing well in a class, take some action. The more seriously you take your education, the better the education will be. A student–instructor relationship is a two-way street. Both parties have responsibilities to make the relationship work. Both sides want to be treated with courtesy and respect. Both sides want successful performance. Both sides must work hard to make the relationship satisfying. If you put the time into building workable relationships with instructors, you will find that you become your own best instructor, because you are in control of your own education.

## How to Get Higher Grades

Most students want high grades, whether for ego satisfaction, for career enhancement, to stay off academic probation, or just for the pleasure of learning a subject and performing well in it. This chapter has discussed so far the way in which your relationship with instructors affects your motivation and learning in a class. The emphasis has been mainly on the instructor's responsibilities in creating a positive atmosphere for learning and techniques you can use to help an instructor do that. The impact of motivation on grades should be clear: the more motivated you are to study in a class, the more likely you are to do well in it.

Your own behaviors also affect your grades in class. You can apply specific techniques to increase the chances of getting high marks. The following suggestions are divided into what you can do before a class begins and what you can do during a class to get higher grades.

1. **Before a class begins, analyze and select carefully.** Use the following techniques to help you select classes:

   - **Do prior research into classes and teachers** to help you avoid poor learning situations and to maximize your internal motivation to do well.

   - **Plan your academic program carefully** so that you do not get trapped in courses or with instructors that you cannot have some choice about.

   - **Register early,** because good instructors and classes usually fill early.

   - **Be persistent** if you are denied entry into a class you really want by talking to the instructor and aggressively letting him know you want in.

   - **Take classes you enjoy** by letting enjoyment be your guide to selecting optional courses to fill general requirements. Do not get trapped in a course simply because you have to fill a requirement.

   - **Take preparatory courses if you have a skills weakness.** If you know you have a lack of skills in some area, take background courses in that area, or consult learning specialists to develop your skills before you take a required class. Do not "wing it" and hope for the best.

   - **Audit especially difficult classes** before enrolling for credit, or plan on taking the course twice to improve your first grade.

   - **Take difficult courses elsewhere** and transfer the credit into your home school. Depending on the course transfer policy of your school, sometimes grades do not transfer in, only course credit. Thus, if you have a low but passing grade in a course taken at another school, you can transfer the credit for the course but avoid having the low grade affect your overall grade average. Research this point with your admissions or records office.

2. **During a class, you can improve your grades.** You can raise the chances for a higher grade by using the following student techniques:

   - **Go to class.** There is a proven statistical correlation between absences and poor classroom performance. The simplest way to ensure high performance is to attend every class. You paid for them, so get your money's worth.

   - **Do the assigned work on time.** Just as attendance is the first and most obvious step toward higher grades, doing the assigned readings and homework will keep you abreast of what is going on in class. If you are not motivated to do the work, analyze the problem and make some changes. If you do not have the time, analyze your schedule and make some changes. If the work is too difficult, analyze your academic program with an adviser and make some changes.

- **Arrive early and stay late.** The best way to build a relationship is to be there. Your chances of talking to the instructor and being organized in the class are increased by taking the extra time.

- **Sit in front.** Instructors remember the names of students who sit in the front, and front-sitters tend to get higher grades. Take advantage of this nonverbal signal that you are interested and willing to be noticed in a class.

- **Be a personality.** Do things so the instructor gets to know you. Volunteer answers and comments. Ask questions. Offer to help or do extra tasks. Talk to the instructor during office hours or before and after class. All these techniques will make you stand out from the crowd and be more involved in your own education. This pays off in higher grades.

- **Take advantage of learning resources.** If the instructor offers voluntary learning methods, make sure you partake. Review sessions, extra projects, volunteer assignments, extra-credit work, additional readings, field trips, or research suggestions offered by the instructor will give you a better grasp of the material and demonstrate to the instructor your willingness and determination to learn.

- **Grapple with the material in a course.** Instead of doing the bare minimum to get by, try to immerse yourself in the subject matter. You will be in college only a short part of your life. Why not take the fullest advantage of it to educate yourself thoroughly, not just on the surface? You may have to sacrifice in areas such as working income, social life, or recreation, but the investment of time in yourself will drastically change the way you perceive the world and the opportunities that become available to you.

## What to Do If You Get a Low Grade

If you get a low grade in a course, do not give up. You have to interpret what that message means. Some students interpret a low grade as a personal evaluation that they are dumb or lazy or worthless. Interpreting low grades personally usually leads to other defeatist behaviors: avoiding talking to the instructor about ways to improve the grade, giving up on making a good grade, dropping the class, or even dropping out of school entirely. Another response is to irrationally blame the instructor for being "too hard" or "too uncaring."

A far more effective approach is to interpret a low grade in a course as a piece of feedback that says, "At present, your skills show a certain level of development." The response to this interpretation is to see the grade as a challenge: what do you have to do to improve your performance? Nothing is personally wrong with you if it is just a matter of improving your skills. After all, that is what college is about: improvement. By seeing grades as signposts toward how to improve, you are much more likely to take the steps that will lead toward improvement, not avoidance.

**Analyze low grades and learn from them.** If you get a low grade in a class, the following techniques will help you confront the underlying issues and plan a strategy for improvement that will lead to higher grades.

- **Look at your study skills.** Did you get the low grade merely because you did not apply yourself and do the work? If so, the solution is simple, unless you have other reasons for not studying.

- **Look at your interests.** Often students do not apply themselves because they are not interested in the course subject matter. The solution here is to be more careful and to select courses that are interesting. You can also try to find things about a course that make it interesting. A good instructor can make any course interesting. It therefore follows that a good student should be able to find things of interest in any course. "Being interesting" is like "beauty": it is in the eye of the beholder. If you want something to be interesting, look for the things that make it relevant and useful for you. Be willing to expand our horizons and try new things.

- **Look at your skill level.** Some low grades are the result of a lack of background for taking a course. If a course is over your head, drop it and take preparatory work that will improve your abilities to perform well in the course later. Not all college courses are for everybody. That is why there are options. Analyze your skills and select courses appropriate for your skill level. Improve your skills, no matter how long it takes (who says college has to be completed in four years?), to master the material you need for the degree.

- **Challenge a surprisingly low grade.** Sometimes instructors do make mistakes in calculating grades. If you think your grade is in error, or if you do not understand how a grade was arrived at, schedule an appointment with your instructor to get an explanation. If it was not a mistake, use the time to develop an action plan for improving your performance in the rest of the course.

- **Discuss an expected low grade.** If you know why your grade was low, discuss your learning problem with the instructor. Discuss what you are doing wrong and determine how you could do it more effectively. You might be able to negotiate a higher grade from the instructor with extra work. If you think the instructor should make changes in the way the course is being run, use your negotiation skills to create some options for better learning and performance. Discuss your study methods and develop an action plan for improving your performance in the class.

- **Offer to redo the work or some alternative.** Many instructors will allow you to redo poor work or do alternative work to improve the final grade in a course. Ask if your instructor has such a policy. Asking in an individual appointment, rather than in front of the entire class, increases the chances of a positive response. You may get turned down, but it does not hurt to ask.

- **Do extra-credit work if it is offered.** Some instructors offer extra-credit assignments as a way for students to improve final grades. If those options are available, take advantage of them. Discuss your ideas for extra-credit early in the course with the instructor. You may be able to tailor the work to fit special interests you have.

## Closing Thoughts

Ultimately, success in college is not dependent upon grades. Real success in college is measured by the usable knowledge you gain, the relationships you build, and the personal growth you attain during your college years. These factors will mold your personality and shape the person you will become in the future. They will also open great opportunities for future personal relationships and careers. Thus, the pursuit of grades should not be your only concern while in school. In fact, if you pursue high grades to the exclusion of everything else, you will miss out on many of the other enriching experiences that college has to offer.

If you do get a low grade in a class, what does that piece of feedback mean to you? Frequently students have unreasonable expectations about high grades. This is a typically American characteristic—to shoot for the moon and hope to win every time! In some situations you will not be a winner, and you must face the consequences of getting a grade lower than you expected. Internalizing the grade as a personal evaluation and quitting the contest by giving up or getting angry are only counterproductive responses. An objective assessment of your study skills, interests, time management, and options to this feedback are much better ways to respond to a low grade. Given these factors, you must decide what is best for you. Some classes are going to be uninteresting. Some fields of study are going to be difficult. Some instructors are going to be impossible to work with. Learning to negotiate tactfully by communicating respectful, positive messages, is an important skill to have in and beyond college. Effective negotiation skills can make the difference in gaining understanding, getting a job, an assignment, a promotion, or a raise.

Competition is not the best learning environment. Far better is a desire for mastery: determining how much you need to know for a specific purpose and applying yourself to your own goals. One of the most important lessons of college is learning to develop your own plan for mastery: finding courses that fit your interests, instructors from whom you want to learn, and relationships that are meaningful to you. Many things can get in the way of this lesson, and you have to learn not to be distracted from your goals.

# Analyzing an Instructor's Style

*Instructions:* Based on the categories discussed in this chapter regarding instructor style, select an instructor from whom you currently are taking a course and analyze his or her style. Select an instructor you particularly enjoy and whose teaching methods work effectively for you.

Instructor analyzed:

Course:

1. What is this instructor's general attitude toward students? What specific things does the instructor do to communicate this attitude?

2. What is this instructor's general attitude toward the subject matter of the class? What specific things does the instructor do to communicate this attitude?

3. How does the instructor demonstrate organizational skills in the class (course outline, assignment deadlines, running class activities, controlling class activity)?

4. Describe the instructor's communication style (interpersonal style, listening skills, public speaking skills, group discussion skills).

5. Describe the instructor's grading practices. Do they seem reasonable and fair? Are they clearly explained in advance?

# Getting To Know an Instructor

*Instructions:* This exercise requires you to meet an instructor whom you do not know. Select an instructor who teaches a course in a major field in which you have some interest. This will be a good way for you to explore possible majors. You can locate a likely instructor by asking your current instructors for recommendations or by checking with departmental secretaries in the major field of your interest. Arrange the interview in the instructor's office during regularly scheduled office hours or at some suitable alternative time. The purpose of the interview is for you to get to know the instructor better and to gain some information about the major or course in which you are interested.

Instructor interviewed:

Department:

1. Purpose of your visit:

2. Courses the instructor teaches:

3. Academic background of the instructor:

4. Why the instructor likes to teach:

5. How the instructor would describe the "ideal student":

6. Information on the major field or course of your interest (courses required, prerequisite skills necessary, career possibilities, etc.):

7. The instructor's suggestions or advice for students in this major:

8. Other questions (use additional pages if necessary):

# Analyzing a Problem Class

*Instructions:* *The purpose of this exercise is to help you analyze a course in which you are having problems. The problem can be small or large, but it should be one that impedes your success in this specific course. Use the suggestions in this chapter for categories in which to describe the instructor's style, your student style, and strategies you can use for coping with the problem in the course.*

Problem course:

Instructor:

1. Describe the problem you are having in this course:

2. Analyze the elements of the instructor's style which might be contributing to this problem:

3. Analyze the elements in your student style that may be contributing to the problem:

4. Discuss the problem with someone else in that class whose opinion you trust, and develop several suggestions for solving the problem:

5. Would you discuss this problem with your instructor and try to negotiate a solution? Why or why not?

## EXERCISE 28

# Negotiating a Problem with an Instructor

*Instructions: Based on your analysis of the problem class in Exercise 27, role play an interview with this instructor by finding a friend to play the role of the instructor. Give the friend your analysis of the problem that you recorded in Exercise 27. In the first role play, have the friend be difficult and uncompromising and see what you can do to find some satisfaction despite this attitude. In the second role play, have the friend play the role much more cooperatively and with a willingness to compromise. See what solutions you can develop in this atmosphere. Have a third student observe you role playing and offer a critique of how you followed the steps.*

Remember the nine steps of successful negotiation:

- Start positively.
- State the overarching goal you both share.
- Explain the obstacle to your success.
- State some alternative solutions you have considered.
- Ask for the instructor's input and opinions.
- Compromise until you find a middle-ground solution.
- Make a commitment to work on the solution.
- Thank the instructor.
- Follow up on the solution reached.

Role Play 1. Describe the interaction you had with the instructor and the results of the interview:

Role Play 2. Describe the interaction you had with the instructor and the results of the interview:

Which of the negotiation skills came easily for you, and which do you need to practice to master?

# 8

## "Why didn't anybody ever tell me?"

One of the worst things that can happen to you in your college career is to get to the final checkout before graduation and then find that you did not take some required course. Surprise! You can't graduate until you take this course, so you have to put everything—your new job, your move out of state, all your plans for post-school life—on hold until you satisfy this requirement. How easy it is to complain, "Why didn't anybody ever tell me?"

One of the major lessons of college is training in the ability to cope with a large, impersonal bureaucracy. If you find yourself in the situation described, you have failed the test! Like any large institution, colleges are regulated by vast numbers of rules and regulations. These were originally designed to make the management of thousands of people more efficient. When they get in the way of what you want, however, just the opposite seems to be the case. They seem designed to thwart you personally.

This chapter will look at methods for learning the lessons of bureaucracy and ensuring that you do not get left in the lurch by a rule or regulation that was waiting to trip you up on the last day. It will review the major advising resources available on campus and offer suggestions on how to use them most effectively.

## Why You Need an Adviser

What does an adviser do? Give advice, right? When do you need advice? When you are confronted by a problem and you need to make a decision. You will face many problems and decisions in college: selecting courses, meeting course requirements, choosing a major, planning a career, finding financial aid, arranging housing, solving relationship problems, taking care of your health, and many others. Most colleges offer a great deal of information about these concerns, so much information, in fact, that the amount of help becomes another problem in itself. Often students are overwhelmed by the information contained in course catalogues, schedules of classes, advice handbooks, and brochures. Honestly speaking, have you read all the materials sent to you by your college?

The time you spend in reading, thinking, and planning about these issues will save you a great deal of trouble and regret later. That is where advisers come in. They help you organize the vast amounts of information confronting you and make sense of it by planning one step at a time. As with most college challenges, following the regulations and meeting requirements is just one more skill you have to master so you do not need someone else's guidance. Until you have gained enough information and savvy to make the best decisions for yourself, however, you need the guidance of advisers, and most colleges provide them in the form of counselors and instructors who are willing to help.

The goal of any advising is to help you reach decisions and take some course of action to solve a problem facing you. This, too, is a major lesson of the college experience: problem solving. Much research has shown that people facing problems and solving them successfully use the same methods again and again. In Chapter 2, you learned the six steps of the critical thinking model. You can also use a similar method for tackling problems. The following Problem-Solving Model should be useful in describing the process and the skills necessary for defining a problem and selecting a best solution. As you read through it, think of a small problem you are facing now, maybe the decision on where to have lunch. Try to apply the steps to your specific problem as you read through the model.

*Problem-Solving Model*

1. **Describe the problem fully:** What is the problem? Where did it come from? Who or what is causing the problem? What is the consequence of the problem? What is not the problem?

2. **Identify possible solutions:** Has anything been tried before? Did it work? Why or why not? What are possible solutions that might work? What are some original or creative approaches to finding solutions? What resources for more information are available?

3. **Develop criteria for the best solution:** Given the present situation, what conditions have to be met for any solution to work? What makes for a good solution or a bad one?

4. **Apply the criteria and find the best solution:** Working through the list of most probable solutions, which one fits the criteria? By process of elimination, which is your best solution?

5. **Apply the solution and watch for results:** When you apply the solution, does it solve the problem? Does it create side effects or new problems that you did not anticipate? Are these worth the value of the solution? If so, do you need to solve the problems caused by the side effects?

Like the critical thinking model, the Problem-Solving Model is useful for small and large problems. Many of the steps can be compacted or even eliminated when the problem is small, because the processes are obvious. When the problem is more complex, however, the model provides a way of structuring the many elements involved in the situation so you can systematically work through the many possibilities, limitations, and variables of the problem situation.

Campus advisers and counselors will use the Problem-Solving Model with you many times as you try to define your problems, identify alternatives, and select the best solutions. It will be useful to familiarize yourself with the process described in the model and prepare for counseling or advising sessions by working through at least the first two steps. Get in the habit of thinking logically about the problems you face. Being aware of the model will help you become solution-oriented and always looking for solutions, rather than problem-oriented, always stumped by the difficulties you meet.

# Advising Resources on Campus

Colleges are filled with people who want to help. Almost any aspect of your life is the specialty of someone on campus who has made it a mission to offer assistance to students who are troubled. The biggest challenge you face is to find the right people when you need them.

The major tool in this process of identifying helpers consists of the **information materials** published by the college. As you went through the application, enrollment, and orientation phases of getting into a college, you were probably inundated with information: pamphlets, brochures, catalogues, handouts, survival guides. Did you read all of it carefully? Most students reply with a resounding "NO!" This response is natural, since at the time there was probably no need for you to read all of that stuff. You were not yet facing any problems that had to be addressed. If you did read any of it, you probably selected the material that addressed specific needs you were aware of at the moment.

Such a response is common sense in an age when we are constantly bombarded with commercial messages and political and social appeals. This natural response can get you into trouble later, however, because you will not have familiarized yourself with the information that can prevent problems from arising or direct you to resources to solve those problems when you run into them. For that reason, it is worth your time to invest an hour or two and carefully review all the materials the college sent to you. Even if you do not need that information at present, you may need it in the future, and it will be helpful for you to know where in the catalogue or in which brochure it is located. Keep these materials stored in an accessible place so when you do need help, you know what is in them and where they are stored.

Most colleges have a system of assigning **academic advisers.** Students routinely ignore these people since they are strangers or are perceived as being too busy. Interestingly enough, the biggest complaint that advisers have is not the vast numbers of students they must handle but the fact that nobody comes to see them! Academic advisers tend to be one of the most underutilized resources on campus. The following section discusses how best to work with your adviser to head off and solve problems as they arise. The key fact to remember is that your adviser is probably your best resource—if you use her. You must take the initiative to build a positive relationship that will work to your advantage as you chart your course through school.

Most colleges have many **additional advising offices** that specialize in particular problems of student life: financial aid, housing, affirmative action, special student status, foreign students, health care, child care. The list of the types of services and advising available on your campus is almost endless. These offices are usually included in some sort of guide to student services (in the information packet you received but didn't read). You should familiarize yourself with all the various types available and fully research their services if you think you may be interested in taking advantage of them. Likewise, if a service you want is not offered, find out which office is most closely related to that service and see if something can be done to provide it. Advisers are willing to help—that is their job—but they need to know what you want done before they can go to work. Exercise 27 at the end of this chapter gives you the chance to locate these offices on your campus.

Another important resource is the **intelligent question.** If you know you have a problem, take the initiative to find help to solve it. One of the major differences between high school and college is the issue of personal responsibility. You are on your own in college much more than ever before, and that means you have to take responsibility for solving your own problems. It does not mean you have to solve them all by yourself; that is what all these helpful resources are about. But you do have to take the first steps to finding and approaching them. The intelligent question—one that shows you have given the issue some thought and tried to find answers on your own but are stumped—is your key to unlocking the vast number of resources available on campus. Perhaps it is best to remember the old adage that there is only one kind of "stupid" question: the one that is not asked. So take the lead in solving your problems by asking questions. Your advisers, your instructors, even your classmates can be useful sources of information if you systematically ask questions to gather the information you need to make good decisions.

The final resource for problem solving is your own habit of **anticipating problems.** Many of the difficulties you will encounter in college could have been avoided if you had anticipated them and planned accordingly. This accounts for the frustration and exasperation you might encounter from some instructors or administrators when you bring a problem situation to them. On the other hand, everybody makes mistakes and some situations cannot be planned for, so take their short-tempered attitudes with a grain of salt and try to make the best of the situation. Being on the lookout for things that can possibly go wrong, listening to other students' problems so you know what to avoid, and talking to your adviser regularly should help you ward off these unfortunate situations.

## Using Your Adviser

The following techniques will help you get the best information and use your time most effectively with your adviser. These same methods can be used when you are talking with an instructor or a special adviser, but they will be addressed here in the academic advising situation.

1. **Meet your assigned adviser.** Before school begins, or during the first weeks of the first term, take the time to arrange an

appointment to introduce yourself to your adviser. You may not yet have any questions to ask or business to transact, but by having met your adviser the first time, you will be more likely to approach him with a question when you do have one. Check out the adviser's personal style just as you do your instructors' styles to see if you will be comfortable working with this person in the coming years. Exercise 31 at the end of the chapter asks you to record your reactions to your academic adviser.

2. **Find your own adviser.** If you do not like the style of your assigned adviser, find another. Most colleges have a system for students to select their own advisers. Research this policy and implement it so you can find an adviser with whom you are comfortable. In many schools, students select their own advisers once they have determined a major. If you know what major you wish to pursue, you may want to choose an adviser in your future field. You will have to go the extra effort to find a list of potential advisers from the department and interview individuals until you find one you like, but the effort will pay off in the long run. Do not let this matter slide by. If you do not like your adviser, find another quickly. Otherwise you may drift through and make costly programming mistakes you will regret.

3. **Know what you want from an adviser.** After the first introductory meeting, it is pointless to go to an adviser unless you have prepared for the interview and have specific questions to which you need answers. You cannot expect an adviser to take hours to help you sort through information that you could digest on your own. Read all the available informative materials about the decisions you have to make, and prepare a set of specific questions for your adviser to answer. In this way, you will be using the adviser's time much more effectively and you will be learning the advising system on your own more quickly.

4. **Check in periodically with your adviser.** Even if you feel confident about understanding the course requirements and selection process in your school, check in with your adviser every term just to have her verify your plans. Advisers will admire the thoroughness of your planning if you have made most of the decisions but still have the foresight to check in with them. There are often many unclear or "hidden" regulations or changes in rules that you might not be aware of that could affect your course planning.

5. **Maintain courtesy and business efficiency with your adviser.** You can facilitate matters and get far better service from your adviser if you show professional courtesy. Call ahead for an appointment rather than dropping by and expecting instant attention. Prepare for the interview and write your specific questions on a checklist rather than expecting the adviser to ask you all the right questions on the spot. If your adviser is particularly helpful, let him know of your appreciation with a kind word at

the end of the interview or a follow-up note. Developing this kind of professional habit of courtesy will serve you well in your future career.

6. **Develop a curriculum plan.** From the very first college term, you should have some idea of where you are going with your college curriculum, all the courses that will add up to your final degree. Even if you are undecided about a major, most colleges have a general education curriculum of background courses in a variety of disciplines that must be taken first. Sit down with the catalogue and begin making decisions about which courses you will want to take to fill these basic requirements. As you select a major, add these new requirements and options to your planning list so you will get some idea of the big picture for the next several years. Having this overview will help you make individual course decisions because you can better see how all the pieces fit together into the whole scheme. You can always change your mind later, but it is good to have at least a preliminary plan that gets you started on the right foot. Exercise 30 at the end of this chapter gives you the chance to start your curriculum plan.

7. **Keep a cumulative record of classes you have taken.** As you advance through school, keep track of all the courses you have taken and the grades you received in them. Note which requirement you have fulfilled with each individual course. Cross-check your cumulative record of courses with your curriculum plan to determine which courses you have yet to take.

8. **Keep your own copies of your records.** Keep a copy of all official correspondence with your college. Errors in records happen, so you want your own records to verify your status. If you receive a special waiver or exception to a requirement, get the person making this decision to write a letter for your own records in case any questions arise later. Keep a copy of the college catalogue for the year in which you enrolled in the school. In most institutions, the requirements of your first year are the ones that will apply to you throughout your college career, so you will want your own copy of that catalogue for your planning.

9. **Take your advising file with you to the adviser.** Assemble your records into an advising file and take it with you every time you go to see your adviser. These documents will help your adviser understand your status and give you better advice. They also demonstrate the seriousness and thoroughness with which you approach your academic career.

## Closing Thoughts

Many of the techniques and suggestions in this chapter have alluded to the bigger lessons that a college degree offers. Ultimately, a college education is more than just a series of courses that educate you in technical knowledge. More important, it consists of a series of relationships and is a measure of how well you have managed those affairs. Thus, learning to cope with a large bureaucracy, taking personal responsibility for your own success, knowing how to analyze and solve problems, being solution-oriented, knowing how to research and find help when it is available, and doing all this with an attitude of professional courtesy are qualities of truly higher education.

If you see your college experience as more than just attending class and getting a degree on paper, perhaps you will be more patient when problems do confront you. Each problem becomes a test of your resourcefulness. Take the time to enjoy and learn from your problems as they occur, for in doing so you will learn these higher lessons that college has to offer.

# Identifying Campus Help Offices

*Instructions:* For each of the student life issue areas listed below, identify the office on your campus that provides information or help. Record the name of the office in which this issue is addressed, the office location, and the phone number for each office. Explore the services of five of them, and briefly describe the services of these five offices.

**Issue**                                **Office Location/Phone/Services**

1. Emergency Medical

2. Police Services (Security)

3. Health/Wellness

4. Housing

5. Financial Aid

6. Career Planning/Placement

7. Stress/Emotional Counseling

8. Lost and Found

| Issue | Office Location/Phone/Services |
|-------|-------------------------------|

9. Computer Training

10. Test-taking Skills

11. Writing Skills

12. Recreation/Athletics

13. Student Newspaper

14. Student Government

15. Student Radio/TV Station

16. Internships/Cooperative
    Education

# Planning Your Curriculum

*Instructions:* *Using the college catalogue for your school, prepare a tentative plan for courses you intend to take during your next four terms (semesters, quarters, trimesters, or whatever). You will probably have many requirements to meet and options to select from, so anticipate that this exercise will take several hours to complete thoroughly. If you do not understand the requirements, prepare a set of questions that you can take to your adviser to have answered. Complete as much of the planning as possible on your own.*

**Courses to Take**      **Reason for Taking (Requirement Met)**

First Term:

| | |
|---|---|
| | |
| | |
| | |
| | |
| | |
| | |
| | |

Second Term:

| | |
|---|---|
| | |
| | |
| | |
| | |
| | |
| | |

**Courses to Take**          **Reason for Taking (Requirement Met)**

Third Term:

|  |  |
|---|---|
|  |  |
|  |  |
|  |  |
|  |  |
|  |  |
|  |  |
|  |  |

Fourth Term:

|  |  |
|---|---|
|  |  |
|  |  |
|  |  |
|  |  |
|  |  |
|  |  |
|  |  |

# Interviewing Your Adviser

*Instructions:* *Identify your academic adviser and arrange an introductory interview if you have not already met this person. In the following form, report on the results of your interview. If you have already met your adviser, plan your first curriculum meeting to have him or her verify your plans for courses you intend to take during your first year in college.*

Adviser's name:

Office location:

Phone:

Office hours:

1. What is your purpose in visiting your adviser? What information do you need? Write out your questions in advance.

2. What is your adviser's style? Did his or her office give you any indication as to the adviser's style?

3. How did the adviser treat you during the interview?

4. What did you discuss in your interview?

5. Did this adviser seem like a person you would be comfortable working with during the school year?

# 9

## "How am I going to pay for school?"

There's no doubt about it—college is expensive. The price of a college education is going up each year. And school costs are not just a matter of tuition and books. You will encounter many hidden costs and unexpected expenses once your college career gets under way. Thus, it is extremely important that you analyze your expenses up front and determine your resources early in your college career so that you can find the ways to finance your education.

Higher education is an investment in your future. A college degree will pay off, but many of you will have to bear the costs of the degree early on, before the investment begins to earn its dividends. According to a recent study, the average U.S. high school graduate can expect to earn $18,737 a year. The average college graduate can expect to earn $32,629 a year. Individual figures vary, of course, but these national averages point out a clear truth—a college degree will open the door to higher income expectations over the rest of your life. And a higher salary is not the only benefit of education. You can also expect a greater range of career choices, more mobility, better chances of advancement in your career, and a higher quality of life in many ways. But you probably know this, which is why you have decided on a college career in the first place.

What you may not know is how you are going to be able to afford this investment. This chapter addresses this issue by leading you through a careful analysis of the three elements of financial management:

- costs, both obvious and hidden, that you will encounter,
- resources, both personal and public, that you can find to assist you, and
- money management strategies to stay on top of your finances.

American college students are fortunate in that almost anyone who has the drive and the talent to gain a higher education can find the means. This is still the land of opportunity, and if you doubt that, you need only look at the stiff, often insurmountable challenges that high school graduates in some countries face to gain access to the benefits of higher education. American institutions, such as state and national student assistance programs, service organizations, and private philanthropic groups, continue the long tradition in American history of helping economically challenged students rise to their highest level of aspiration. They know that everyone—not just the student but the whole country—will benefit from every citizen being given the greatest chance possible to make the most of his life. That is why over $3 billion a year is awarded to college students. Your challenge now is to find your share of that massive self-improvement effort.

## The Costs of Your Education

The first step in getting control of your financial picture is to arrive at a realistic estimate of your current and future expenses. Exactly how much will college cost you? The following categories illustrate the many kinds of costs you will encounter:

- tuition and fees—the costs of attending classes, laboratories, and using college facilities;
- books and supplies—textbooks, workbooks, additional reading and studying materials, laboratory and art supplies, writing and office materials;
- lodging—dormitory expenses, rent if living independently or contributing to home costs;

- food—meal plan, snacks, groceries, meals;
- transportation—travel expenses to and from school and during the school term (if you maintain your own car, include gas, maintenance and repairs, insurance, car payment, fees, and parking);
- entertainment—special meals out, sporting/cultural events, movies, dating expenses, pleasure reading, party expenses;
- personal expenses—clothing, recreation, health supplies and services, telephone, laundry, toiletries/cosmetics, gifts (these are expenses you would incur even if not in school but they must be calculated just the same);
- additional costs—depending upon your personal circumstances, these could include travel or study abroad, child care, special services for disabled students, special medical expenses.

It is difficult to be totally accurate when estimating costs for a college education that will span several years, because many variables affect these estimates. For one thing, costs will inflate the longer you attend school—tuition, fees, cost of books and personal expenses will continue to rise. A second factor is that most people tend to underestimate their real costs of living. For example, how much would you estimate that you spend annually on entertainment? Make a wild guess. It is estimated that the average college student spends between $800 and $1,000 a year on entertainment. Was your estimate that high? Probably not, but if you kept a careful account of your spending, you would begin to see the problem. Everything costs more than you expect it to, and all categories of your expenses are affected by this perception.

It is extremely important that you determine your costs up front as accurately as possible in order to get a clear picture of your financial commitments. A useful tool for doing this is an **allowance schedule** in which you calculate anticipated costs and then commit yourself to staying within the allowance you set up for each category. To illustrate, using our example of entertainment, if you create an allowance of $80 a month ($720 for a nine-month school year), that means that you must stick to that limit—$20 a week—if you are going to keep within your allowance for that item.

Some allowance items are easier to stick to than others. **Fixed costs** that will not fluctuate within a given year, such as tuition or the cost of room and board in a dorm, help you anticipate exact costs for these items. **Variable costs,** such as entertainment or food if you are living in an apartment, will fluctuate—usually higher than your expectations. This is why many students find it easier to create as many fixed costs and to avoid as many variable costs as possible in their allowance schedules. Fixed costs will remain the same and can be anticipated and planned for. Variable costs, if they get out of control, can wreck your budget and disrupt your financial planning.

Exercise 32 at the end of this chapter asks you to develop a tentative personal allowance schedule for your first year of school (two semesters or three quarters roughly from September to May). Check local information sources to determine fixed costs such as tuition, fees, and dorm rates. Estimate the variable costs as realistically as you can. Once you have developed this part of your personal budget, sit down with someone whose opinion you trust and analyze it carefully by asking yourself the following questions. Have you anticipated all the real costs? Have you estimated variable costs realistically? Are there places where you can economize if you need to lower your expenses?

Once you have analyzed and corrected your allowance schedule, the bottom line is your anticipated yearly cost of your college education. Is it more than you expected? Now comes the challenge of finding the resources to pay for it. Facing the **bottom line** of a personal budget is often intimidating, since we are usually unaware of exactly how much it takes to keep us going. Perhaps this exercise will help you appreciate one of the challenges of being a parent. We often take for granted the outlay in resources it takes to raise, clothe, and educate a child. Creating a personal budget may give you some insight into this challenge when you suddenly become responsible for your own finances.

## Strategies For Locating Financial Resources

There you have it—the bottom line is staring you in the face. How are you going to pay for it? You have many resources available to you. Some of them you may not be aware of, so it is important to research all the possible avenues and take advantage of every one.

Digging for resources is the dirty, un-fun part of budget planning. Filling out forms, investigating grants and loans, filling out more forms, interviewing people who may be of possible assistance, and filling out even more forms is not fun work. It takes time and effort to pursue these avenues of funding, and you have to stick to the effort in order to make it work. Many students get discouraged about the effort and unpleasantness involved, but look at it this way. If you could work just two weeks and get all the money you need to finance an entire year of school—$5,000, $10,000 or $20,000 or whatever—would you be willing to invest that much time? Most people don't hesitate to say "Yes!" Two weeks is 80 working hours. As you begin the process of investigating resources, put a chart above your bed, in your wallet, or in some other conspicuous place, and jot down the time you have spent every time you spend an hour or two talking to a financial counselor, filling out a form, interviewing a possible contributor to your education, or applying for a loan. Keep track of exactly how much time you are putting into the effort of financing your education. Eighty hours of work will produce amazing results. Few students require even half that amount of time to find the resources they need. By keeping track of your efforts, however, you will begin to see that you are just putting in the hours it takes to find the necessary resources.

There are many possible sources of funding for you to explore, but before we get into the specifics of possible sources, here are a few basic strategies to keep in mind:

- **Investigate personal resources first.** Look to relatives, your own employment, and personal savings for your best possible sources of funding. If these are limited, then consider other avenues.

- **Always apply for everything that you are eligible for.** Every year, millions of dollars of financial aid go unclaimed and unawarded because nobody applied for them. Do not let this happen to you. Talk to a financial adviser, find out what you are eligible for, and make sure that you apply. If you have surplus personal funds, bank them for a rainy day.

- **Consider a "pool" approach to funding.** Do not expect all your funding to come from one source. Look for many possible sources to contribute to your financial pool. That way, if one source dries up, there are other sources still flowing.

- **Consult with your local financial adviser.** Most schools provide professional advice on financial planning. These offices are often horribly institutionalized—long lines, endless forms to fill out, frazzled nerves, and lots of waiting. But remember your 80-hour commitment. Take a book to read, strike up conversations with other people, and chalk up the waiting to your two weeks of research. The waiting and form-filling are usually worth the effort.

- **Maintain contact with your financial adviser.** Do not think that all your financial planning can be done before the start of just your freshman year. Finding resources should be a constant activity during your college career. Remember, the more time you put into the search, the greater the rewards will probably be. Stay in touch with your financial adviser, and constantly explore new possibilities for funding.

- **Apply early for financial aid.** Do not wait until the last minute to apply for the coming year. Investigate the time deadlines and get applications in early. The sooner you get to the task, the more possibilities you open for yourself. As part of the application procedure, determine the time lag between submitting the paperwork and the actual payout of funds. These time delays can vary tremendously depending on the school and the kind of award. Do not get caught short because you are waiting for money that will not arrive until later than you expect.

- **Keep records of everything you do.** You may find yourself frustrated by filling out forms because they all seem to be asking for the same information. Make it easy on yourself by keeping a **master financial file** of all your personal records—bank account numbers, names and addresses of references, income statements, tax forms, grant and loan applications, etc. Filling out forms is a breeze if you have all the data you need right at your fingertips. Make a copy of everything you submit and you will not ever have to do the same work twice.

The following list describes the three basic forms of financial assistance for students:

---

*Types of Available Financial Aid*

- **scholarships/grants**—gift awards you do not have to pay back as long as you fulfill the terms of qualification (e.g. full-time enrollment, athletic/artistic performance, grade point average, etc.);
- **loans**—money that must be paid back at some point;
- **work–study**—income you earn through part-time employment programs specially designed for students.

---

Each school offers various forms of each of these three kinds of financial assistance. The best strategy for you is to talk to a financial adviser at your school. You need to determine which kinds of assistance you qualify for and make the appropriate applications.

Scholarships and grants can be awarded on the basis of financial need, special fields of study, high scholastic aptitude, athletic or artistic aptitude, parental membership in social or fraternal organizations, and competitions in such skills as public speaking or writing. Libraries, bookstores, and financial aid offices offer several good guides to available scholarships and directories of financial aids for women, minorities, and general students. A financial aid counselor should also be able to fill you in on which local scholarships and grants (offered by your school, your state, or by private organizations) and federal grants (such as the Federal Pell Grants and Educational Opportunity Grants) you are eligible to apply for. A separate application is often required for each grant, so you can expect to be filling out lots of forms. Keep copies of each application to make this process easier.

Loans also come in many forms. The most common are the following:

- Federal Perkins Loan
- Federal Stafford Loan

- Unsubsidized Federal Stafford Loan
- Federal Supplemental Loans for Students (SLS)
- Federal Parental Loans for Undergraduate Students (PLUS)

The terms of qualification, interest, and payback vary in each of these loans. You should check with your financial adviser for the specific details of these programs.

One thing to keep in mind about loans is that ultimately you will have to repay them. Try not to rely solely on loans to finance your education. It can be difficult to start a career if you are facing massive debts once you graduate from school. Try to keep loans to a minimum and apply for them only in emergency situations when your other sources of funding dry up. Keep in mind that your frugal student lifestyle may have to continue for several years after school if you have amassed a big loan debt.

Many schools have tried to simplify grant and loan application procedures by requiring only a single application form, often the Free Application for Federal Student Aid (FAFSA). This single application may only cover certain grant and loan possibilities, so make sure that you investigate all your possible sources of funding and submit separate applications when required.

Work–study programs, such as the Federal Work–Study (FWS), provide part-time employment to students. These jobs often are in convenient on-campus departments and offices and in academically related tasks. A separate application may be necessary to participate in this program. Investigate your local financial aid office for more information. Many schools also offer general part-time employment services such as job listings, placement services, job lead boards, and job-finding services. Check out these local resources, too.

Beyond grants, loans, and work–study programs, you need to investigate your personal resources:

- **Relatives and friends**—consider approaching these people with a request for support of your education. Remember the "pool" approach—many people giving small amounts can add up.

- **Off-campus, part-time employment**—some jobs in the community may pay more than work-study programs and offer better hours.

- **Summer employment**—by keeping expenses down and working through the summer, many students can finance an entire year of school.

- **Year-off employment**—while it interrupts your educational career, some students find it necessary to work full-time periodically in order to save for a return to school.

- **Self-employment**—enterprising students can supplement their incomes by providing special services to other students such as typing, disk-jockeying for parties, jewelry and crafts sales, piano tuning, and so on.

Once you have thoroughly investigated all your possible resources, you need to list them and compare them to your costs. Exercise 33 asks you to do this for the coming school year. The bottom-line cost figure you calculated in Exercise 32 needs to be balanced by the bottom-line resources figure in Exercise 33. If there is a short-fall in resources, how are you going to balance the account? This is where good financial advice comes in.

Talk to your relatives, friends whose judgment you trust, or a financial adviser at your school to see if you have considered all your options. There may be avenues for funding that you are not aware of and have left untouched.

## Tips for Managing Your Personal Finances

Taking on the commitment of getting a college education often means sacrifice. At first the idea of sacrifice may seem like loss— you are losing old conveniences, habits, and pleasures. You may have to give up things to which you have grown accustomed. But in another way sacrifice is freedom—you become free to find a new life and grow beyond your old way of being.

Within the last few years, several famous people experienced life changing events to which they responded heroically. Baseball player Brett Butler was diagnosed with cancer, underwent 33 radiation treatments, and returned to hit the winning run for his team in his first game back. A serious accident on board her band's tour bus broke singer Gloria Estefan's back. She dedicated herself to a full recovery and later performed at the closing ceremonies of the 1996 Summer Olympic Games in Atlanta. After actor Christopher Reeve was paralyzed in a horseback riding accident, he continually worked to extend his abilities. He was a speaker at the 1996 Democratic National Convention in Chicago. An on-court stabbing caused Monica Seles to take time off from tennis to recover from her physical and emotional injuries. She returned to tennis to win the Australian Open.

The way you think about financial sacrifice has a lot to do with how easily you can adapt to a new, more demanding environment. As you consider how you will balance college costs and resources, keep in mind that sacrifice is not all bad. It may be the chance for you to change and experience new ways of living and experiencing the world.

The following suggestions are some ways in which students have managed to control their personal finances and keep costs under control.

- **Maintain a personal budget.** Keep regular accounts of expenses and income. At regular intervals analyze your expenses to see if they are getting beyond your allowances.

- **Find part-time work related to your educational goals.** If at all possible, work in ways that will contribute to your long-term plans. Find jobs that develop skills and contacts that will be of use to you later as well as help pay the short-term bills. Part-time jobs are excellent ways to explore possible career directions.

- **Control books and supplies costs.** Buy used books when you can, and sell back books at the end of the school term. Books quickly go out of date, so unload them as soon as you can.

- **Control living expenses**—lodging and food—by considering communal living. College dormitories and dining halls are usually cheaper than living independently. Weigh carefully the costs, benefits, and disadvantages of dorms, independent living, and living at home and commuting.

- **Keep transportation costs low.** The maintenance on an automobile can be a large expense. Consider selling or storing your car for a year and experiment with life in the pedestrian lane. Car pooling can cut commuting costs significantly. Most residential colleges discourage students from having a car and are especially designed for foot traffic. This can be a great savings.

- **Control your personal costs.** An important tip in this area is to make cash purchases only. Do not get in the habit of charging on credit cards. Delay purchases whenever you can. Impulse buying can wreck a budget. Shop for bargains when you must buy items. The bottom line is—stop buying stuff.

The best piece of advice for maintaining your budget while you are in school is to realize that you will probably have to scale back your expectations as a consumer. You may not have noticed it, but Americans tend to place high status and measure personal worth by the amount of money they have to spend on consumer goods. If you are financially challenged to pay for a higher education, this is a perfect opportunity to challenge this notion of rampant consumerism in your own life. Do not drag along all the baggage of your old lifestyle. Live well, but do it cheaply. Prove to yourself that you do not need buckets of money to be happy. Exercise 34 gives you the chance to play with this notion. Find free fun. Plan your life out of a single suitcase. Find a hero to serve as an inspiration through this time of sacrifice. The insights you gain from this control of your finances will change how you look at the world.

## Closing Thoughts

College students easily fall into the "way it's supposed to be" trap. Somewhere along the way, the expectation got established that a college education meant four years of extended childhood—starting the fall after high school graduation, with summer breaks for working at camp or as a lifeguard or in some other low-paying recreational pursuit, with college life full of parties and nights out, with someone else magically footing the bill.

The reality of our world is that most students will not experience college that way. They may have to delay college for a year or two to raise the funds, take periods off to work or to raise children, go to school at night or during the summer to accelerate their programs or maintain a full-time job, and live frugally in order to make ends meet. Does that make their experience any less valuable or less complete than the "traditional" way of financing a college education? Of course not. If anything, great experience and self-growth can be gained from this sacrifice. There is no "right" way of gaining an education. Every person's college degree will consist of years of experiences that are totally her own unique odyssey.

Ultimately, financing your education is just another of the "life lessons" that you gain from the college experience. Your creativity, resourcefulness, and tenacity will be put to the test. But this testing is the only way in which you can also learn these skills. The lessons you learn in calculating costs and resources, living within your means, and being in control of your personal finances will stand you in good stead throughout the rest of your life.

If you are financially challenged while attending school, do not short-change your experience just because it is not based on a box of cash. College life is full of rich experience just waiting to be discovered. All it takes is the time and courage to look in places you would not usually look, to talk to people who are different from those whom you already know, and to stretch your horizons by thinking and experimenting with new ideas. These are the things that make life rich, and college is just the first step on this journey.

# Calculating Your College Costs

*Instructions:* *Complete the following allowance schedule for your first year of college. Estimate your costs in the following categories. Be as realistic and complete as possible. Calculate a bottom line cost for the school term. You may need to do some research for specific cost factors.*

| School term: | Fall | Winter | Spring | Summer | Totals |
|---|---|---|---|---|---|
| Tuition/fees | _____ | _____ | _____ | _____ | _____ |
| Books/supplies | _____ | _____ | _____ | _____ | _____ |
| Lodging | _____ | _____ | _____ | _____ | _____ |
| Food | _____ | _____ | _____ | _____ | _____ |
| Transportation | _____ | _____ | _____ | _____ | _____ |
| Personal expenses | _____ | _____ | _____ | _____ | _____ |
| Entertainment | _____ | _____ | _____ | _____ | _____ |
| Additional costs: | _____ | _____ | _____ | _____ | _____ |
| **BOTTOM LINE:** | _____ | _____ | _____ | _____ | _____ |

Once you have calculated your costs, analyze places in which you think you might be able to reduce costs. Outline below three areas in which you may be able to reduce the estimates of costs.

*Cost Saving Idea #1:*

*Cost Saving Idea #2:*

*Cost Saving Idea #3:*

## EXERCISE 33

# Determining Your Financial Resources

*Instructions:* *For the coming school year, list all of the resources you have available. Discuss your list of resources with a financial adviser. Carefully investigate any possible sources of funding that you may have overlooked.*

| School term: | Fall | Winter | Spring | Summer | Totals |
|---|---|---|---|---|---|
| Scholarships/ Grants | _____ | _____ | _____ | _____ | _____ |
| | _____ | _____ | _____ | _____ | _____ |
| | _____ | _____ | _____ | _____ | _____ |
| | _____ | _____ | _____ | _____ | _____ |
| | _____ | _____ | _____ | _____ | _____ |
| Loans: | _____ | _____ | _____ | _____ | _____ |
| | _____ | _____ | _____ | _____ | _____ |
| | _____ | _____ | _____ | _____ | _____ |
| Personal Sources: | _____ | _____ | _____ | _____ | _____ |
| | _____ | _____ | _____ | _____ | _____ |
| | _____ | _____ | _____ | _____ | _____ |
| **BOTTOM LINE:** | _____ | _____ | _____ | _____ | _____ |

With a group of students or with a financial adviser, discuss possible avenues for increasing your resources. Make an action list of things you want to follow up on in the areas:

*Local Financial Aid Office:*

*Scholarships/Grants:*

*Loans:*

*Personal Sources:*

# Thinking Creatively About Finances

*Instructions: Just to stretch your limits about how you view yourself as a consumer, complete the following three parts of this exercise—just for fun.*

Part 1: Free Fun. List all the ways you can think of entertaining yourself (by yourself or with your family, a friend, or a date) that do not cost anything. Once you have completed this list, share and compare with other students.

Part 2: Life From a Single Suitcase. Until only recently, college students often went off to school with only a single suitcase for their belongings. Imagine that your packing for school was limited to just a single suitcase. What would you include? And what did you consciously leave out?

| Items To Include | Items to Leave Out |
| --- | --- |
| | |
| | |
| | |
| | |
| | |
| | |
| | |
| | |
| | |

Part 3: Finding a Hero. Think of some character—a hero on a great adventure—in fiction or film or history who best exemplifies how you would like to see yourself at college. What are the challenges that this person faces? How did he or she overcome these challenges? What resources did he or she have? How are you going to emulate this person?

# 10

## "Why are these other people so weird?"

The college experience is full of emotional adjustments that come as a surprise to most students. Invariably, college is different from what most people expect it to be. When a student is open to the many opportunities available, college is much more challenging and life-changing than bargained for. When a student is not interested in challenge or change, however, college becomes far less interesting.

One of the biggest challenges and emotional adjustments required of students who enter college immediately after high school is having to interact on an adult level with people who are far different—even radically different—from them. For most students, high school was a fairly homogeneous experience. High school students tend to form friendship groups with others who are similar to them, if not in racial and ethnic ways, then certainly in standards of economic level and social aspirations.

Most colleges set a goal for their students to be much more individual in their adult relationships. The unusually diverse student populations of many colleges force students to interact with others who have entirely different backgrounds, customs, social behaviors, social expectations, and even languages. This individual responsibility to interact effectively with people who are different creates tension and problems. It is awkward and difficult to get to know and come to appreciate people who are so different from oneself.

The American university fulfills a mission in our culture as the great equalizer for the various types of people that constitute American society. Likewise, a college education is perceived universally as the great opportunity for people to better themselves and raise their lots in the world. Because of these missions, colleges are committed to **equality**—treating people with respect for their differences—and **opportunity**—giving people the chance to perform at their highest levels as individuals.

The awkwardness and difficulty of accepting and interacting with people who are different from ourselves runs directly counter to these goals of equality and opportunity. The intensity of work demanded at the college level requires an awareness and acceptance, not just toleration, of difference. The emphasis on individuality requires respect, not just a lack of bias or prejudice.

This chapter explores these issues in terms of the specialness of individuals. It looks at some of the challenges that arise from cultural diversity and some ways of helping students meet the challenges of awareness, acceptance, and respect when dealing with people who are different from themselves.

## Who Is a Special Student?

In how many ways can you divide a hundred college students into groups? Think for a moment. If you were to have 100 diverse college students in a room, how many different groups can you think of into which the students could be separated. Jot down in the following space all the various groups you can think of.

The most obvious groups, of course, are the ones with visible characteristics: race, gender, visible physical disability, age, size, hair color, and so on. More subtle are the cultural and values differences: economic level, ethnicity, political ideology, religion, sexual orientation. Invisible internal differences include factors such as intelligence, personality traits, attitudes, abilities, social interests, and learning disabilities. Another way to divide people would be by a specific behavioral characteristic: where they live, how they get to school, whether they work while attending school, the language they speak at home, or the academic program in which they are enrolled. How many of these categories did you think of initially? Probably many more could be added to the list.

As you can see, students could be separated into many different types of groups. Once you start combining groups and subdividing even further, the permutations become almost endless. For example, taking only the first category in each division above, you could have the Asian, rich, smart, apartment dwellers in the first subdivision, and so on. Each one of these subdivisions has unique interests and needs. Some are so commonplace that they have developed a social identity. Others are so refined that only one in a million students might fit that category.

The point of this discussion is to demonstrate that once you start dividing people into groups and treating them as members of "a group," you begin to destroy the individuality and unique personal differences of each person. Of course, groups are important. We share with other people certain visible characteristics, cultural values, internal qualities, and behaviors. These similarities give us a sense of security and belonging. But overemphasizing the group to which a person belongs denies the specialness of each individual. Additionally, any one person is going to belong to many different subgroups. Overemphasizing only one group characteristic or behavior does not give credit for the many other qualities that person might have.

Thus, there is a tension in the college community. How much emphasis should be placed on the needs of groups? And how much emphasis should be placed on the needs of unique individuals? Should certain groups be given special treatment because of their group character? Is it right to treat someone differently just because she is a member of a certain group? Should all students be treated exactly the same, with no consideration of their special group needs? Is a college inherently unequal when most of its faculty are members of one particular group? Is it possible for people in different groups to ever really understand one another? Is it better for groups to live separately and try to respect each other, or is separateness inherently unequal? These questions lead to many problems on the campus.

# Understanding the Specialness of Others

These issues have no easy solutions or they would not be as volatile as they are today. A way to begin finding solutions, however, is to focus on the interpersonal dynamics of people in groups, how people try to understand and communicate with each other. Three major processes surface as ways to find solutions to problems that emerge from cultural diversity: awareness, acceptance, and respect.

**Awareness** is the process of realizing that people are affected to some degree by the groups of which they are members. Historically, the American social ideal was assimilation, the melting pot theory of everybody shedding group characteristics and becoming uniquely "American." The trouble with this theory was in defining what American was. Each group tends to think its own standards, behaviors, values, and experiences are the best and truest measure for determining that. A better way of dealing with people is to realize they are affected by their group backgrounds and to respect those backgrounds, but also to realize that most group members have cross-over values and behaviors that they share with other groups. These shared values become the basis for understanding and social cohesion. The great challenge in American culture is for groups to learn to respect each other's differences and find commonalities they can agree upon, not for everyone to try to agree on everything.

**Acceptance** is the process of withholding judgment about differences. It is a human characteristic to place positive value on (to like, prefer, be attracted to) the things that are similar to ourselves and to devalue (to blame, condemn, or ridicule) things that are different from ourselves. Think for a moment of your childhood. Were you ever ridiculed for something that was different about you? Groups have a way of maintaining conformity (therefore, social cohesion and control) by using ridicule and blame to keep "deviant" members in line. This process in groups often runs amok and does more harm than good. It requires exceptional maturity for an individual not to be threatened by differences and to be willing to withhold judgment until all the factors in a situation are understood fully. For the process of open communication to work among groups, an atmosphere of acceptance must be established; otherwise, emotions will cloud the picture and the reasonable discussion of issues cannot occur.

**Respect** is the process of coming to see the value in other people, even if they are different from ourselves in significant ways, and communicating our perception of value to them in terms they understand. Respect is not just a passive mental appreciation. It requires the conscious acts of resisting prejudgment, looking for things of value in others, and actively communicating our feelings of admiration for qualities or behaviors in others. Respect is not a common trait of Americans. Our competitive consumer culture is fueled mainly by messages of disrespect: "You are not pretty enough, rich enough, thin enough, classy enough, macho enough, or important enough. All you have to do is buy our product and we will fix that for you." You have to work at and purposively learn to be respectful of others or respect will not happen. Fortunately, respect becomes a self-fulfilling prophecy. Once you learn to respect others, you begin to respect yourself more and others begin to show you greater respect.

These three processes are not easy to learn. Many aspects of our culture inhibit us from grasping these lessons. Groups still tend to isolate themselves from one another, so individuals are not aware of what people in other groups are actually like. News media and competitive politicians tend to focus on the problems that groups have and the things that divide groups of people who are different, rather than looking at the common values and goals that people in different groups share. Current trends in group pride movements often isolate a group even more from other groups around it instead of fostering open avenues of acceptance. Demands for special treatment because of unique group needs often lead to inter-group jealousy, not understanding. The lack of training in respect in our culture leads to internalized feelings of low self-esteem manifested in family and public violence, substance abuse, and other forms of self-destructive behavior.

If you are concerned about becoming more accepting and respectful of other people and their cultures, you have to set specific goals and work toward that end. In looking at the problems created by cultural insensitivity, both on a national as well as an individual level, you may see the need for this training more clearly. Unfortunately, it is hard to find this kind of training in a culture that thrives on competitive exclusivity.

## The Problems Created by Cultural Insensitivity

It is easy to shrug off these issues by saying, "Oh well, there will always be problems out there. Fortunately, my life is in pretty good shape." By looking at the common problems on campus resulting from a lack of awareness, acceptance, and respect, you may begin to see how pervasive the problems are, even in your own realm of experience. The following examples are drawn from real college students' experiences. Can you add your own observations or experiences to the list?

1. **Avoidance.** The most common problem in group interaction is that people tend to avoid members of groups different from themselves. They usually have lots of rationalizations for this avoidance: "It's too awkward to walk up and start talking to someone I

don't know" or "I don't know what to say." Of course it is awkward to walk up to someone and say, "Hey, you look like a lesbian. Tell me, what's it like to be a lesbian?" or to confront someone in the cafeteria with, "Say, you're black, right. I'm doing a sociology project, so tell me, what's it like to be black?" Any member of any group would be put off by these unnatural and artificial approaches. Avoidance becomes a real problem when the opportunity to interact naturally is there but resisted. You have to work actively at getting to know people who are different from yourself. If you do not get to know someone different when the opportunity does arise, when will you ever meet people you do not already know? Opportunities in the typical college setting include the following:

- striking up a conversation in an elevator or while standing in line;
- saying hello to strangers as you walk along the street;
- selecting partners for class projects or study teams;
- asking for assistance when you need to ask a question;
- making eye contact with people in a class;
- choosing people with whom to strike up a friendship.

There are hundreds of opportunities for people to interact either on a short-term, shallow level or on a more long-term, deeper level. Look at your own behavior. Do you avoid people of groups different from yourself, or does that consideration cross your mind as you interact daily?

2. **Lack of familiarity with different cultures.** If you do not know anything about what it is like to be an international student, or the challenges disabled people face, or the special needs of single parents who are going to school, you are missing out on a vital component of the college experience. Your opportunity to meet these people and share the common experience of college life is unlike any other opportunity you probably will have in life. The skeptic will say, "Yeah, but why should I bother?" There are two reasons. First, it will not happen unless you make it happen. You have to work at cultural understanding or it will not develop in you. Second, the insight and experiences in human interaction you will gain from getting to know and respect people from different groups are skills that will be useful to you throughout your life. Concerns relating to cultural difference pervade every aspect of the world. If you become skilled dealing with them now, you will be much better equipped to handle them in later life, whether on the job, in personal relationships, or in thinking about national social problems and issues.

3. **Insensitivity to other people's needs.** When other people say they are concerned about something, one of the worst things you can say to them is, "Well, I just don't see why that is such a

problem. It isn't a problem for me." People in different groups have different backgrounds and different needs. They see the world differently. They emphasize different values, and they place value on different things. What they like or what upsets them is different from what you may like or what might upset you. When someone who is different from you expresses a concern or a need, try to understand where the person is coming from. If you do not understand, ask questions. Start the process of awareness. Carefully withhold value statements implying that your perceptions or experience or values are the "right" ones. Opening yourself to communication with someone is the best way to understand that person and for him or her to understand you. The sensitivity you learn in dealing with others who are different from you will help you tremendously in all the relationships in your life. We often assume that people who are similar to us in many ways are similar in all ways, and that is often not the case. Sensitivity means carefully looking for information and withholding biases that impede an objective view. It is a valuable tool for anyone.

4. **Treating people as representatives of a group.** As human beings, we are caught in the tension between being a member of a group and being an individual. It is good to be proud of the group to which you belong and to share common values and experiences with others who are similar to you. It is also good to be valued as an individual, unique and unlike anyone else in the world, with fears and aspirations that are yours alone. To be sensitive to one another, we have to be sensitive both to the group and the individual aspects of that person. As we have discussed, cultural awareness means understanding how a person is affected by the group to which he belongs. On the other hand, you should be aware of individual differences, too. It is easy to fall into the trap of stereotyping and overgeneralization when talking about group characteristics, traits, or behaviors. For the most part, these generalizations are false and, often, insulting. When dealing with people of different groups, it is important also to respect their individual differences and not make assumptions or conclusions on the basis of a person's group affiliations. This is what makes cultural sensitivity so difficult. You have to be sensitive to the culture and to the individual at the same time. The interaction of these two variables is often inconsistent, confusing, and emotionally laden. But that's what being human is all about.

5. **Making value judgments of people.** Whenever someone does something of which we do not approve, we commonly label that person with badness terms: evil, selfish, cruel, perverted, lazy, stupid, and so on. Likewise, people having behaviors of which we approve we label with goodness terms: right, generous, natural, industrious, smart, and so on. This process of valuing and labeling equates the *person* with the *behavior of the person.* This is a form of

overgeneralization that impedes communication because it usually makes the one being labeled defensive and retaliatory. This process of labeling occurs often among people in different groups, and it interferes with open communication. A far better way of handling disagreements over values is to explore sympathetically and understand why the behavior exists, objectively describe the consequences of the behavior, and rationally negotiate solutions for preventing or solving the problem. When reinforced by the sensitivity methods of awareness, acceptance, and respect, this becomes a means for handling differences in values and opinions. (In a system of laws and rules, even when a decision is made that is contrary to a person's values, there are ways to go about changing the rules. This system makes for constant struggle and change, often not a comfortable way to live. But in a larger sense, there is great optimism in this atmosphere as long as people believe that ultimately the best for everyone will prevail. The only alternative is anarchy and the rule of the most powerful.) On an individual level, a person should resist using emotionally loaded labels. Instead, respect for difference comes when you objectively explore causes, behaviors, and effects and work toward a mutually satisfying solution. Using language more sensitively and carefully makes the process of cultural sensitivity much easier.

## Techniques for Becoming More Sensitive to Cultural Differences

This chapter has suggested several general techniques for becoming more sensitive to people of cultures that are different from yours. You might consider several additional methods as you expand your awareness and acceptance of people who are different from you.

1. **Be aware of your own group identities.** On the walls of the Delphic oracle in ancient Greece was carved the motto that guided the wisdom of the old world: "Know thyself." This is a good place to begin a college career in the modern world. It is vital to be aware of how you—your attitudes, values, customs, goals, and behaviors—are a product to some extent of the cultural group in which you were reared. If you had been born into a different group, how might some of those elements have been different? It is also a positive sign to be proud of the valuable qualities of groups to which you belong, but not to have blind pride and see good only in your own group. Finally, it is important to realize that you are a member of many culturally diverse groups, and you constantly will be entering new groups as you move through life. Right now, you have entered the ranks of "college student," as in the phrase "Oh, it's just those crazy college students demonstrating again." This is a unique category in American culture. Are you

aware of the privileges and responsibilities entailed in the membership of this new group? Your group allegiances will expand and overlap with other people with whom you never would have thought you had anything in common. As this happens, you will see that people have many more things in common than they have different. It is all a matter of what you choose to look at.

2. **Seek out people who are different from you.** Whenever you have to meet new people, do not fall victim to the avoidance behaviors that keep you isolated and narrowly focused in your own familiar perspective. You can learn many valuable lessons in human dynamics from getting to know and accepting people who have a different way of looking at the world. With classmates, with co-workers, with instructors and administrators, take the time to understand their cultural orientation and how that makes them different from you. Take the risk of getting to know someone different.

3. **Find advisers who are sensitive to your unique needs.** Everyone needs a friendly and sympathetic shoulder to lean on when the going gets rough. Look for advisers who understand what it is like to be the special person you are and the special group to which you belong. If you are lucky, your school will have addressed this issue by creating programs for special groups, such as culture centers, special advising programs, ethnic studies counselors, programs for returning students, specially identified counselors for groups with specific needs, mentorship programs, women's centers, and international student offices. Use the resources of these programs if they have been created. They often have to justify their existence by the numbers of students for whom they provide service. If these programs do not exist at your school, perhaps you can start a movement to get them going by talking to a concerned faculty member or administrator.

4. **Talk to professors about your special concerns.** Instructors are only human, too, and they often err in being less than sensitive to cultural differences. If you have an instructor you think is not being sensitive to your needs, negotiate or her about the difficulty that is affecting your learning. As with any instructor problem, it may not do any good, but at least you will have begun the work needed to finally get some change in the system. You might be surprised to find how aware instructors are of the impact that cultural difference has in their classes and how willing they are to talk about it. Discussing problems is the first step in solving them. It is up to you to start the process if you feel there is a problem regarding lack of sensitivity.

5. **Confront covert and overt cultural prejudices.** Instructors and students sometimes make unintentional or covert cultural prejudgments or put-downs, not knowing how strongly these might affect other people. If you are offended by something another person does or says that you think violates the standards

of sensitivity that professionals should exhibit, say something. It takes courage to voice an opinion that may not be popular or attuned to a group's "in thinking," but you will feel better for having done it. Perhaps the discussion your complaint provokes will do some good in helping people to become more aware and sensitive. Likewise, if a person is behaving in an overtly prejudiced or biased way, politely point out how you differ in opinion. By all means, if an instructor is making sexist or racist or other biased comments, let your opinions be known—first to the instructor in a private negotiating session and then with higher authorities if that does no good. Most institutions of higher learning have a strong commitment to equality and respect and will support you totally if your complaint is justified.

## Closing Thoughts

When all is said and done, all individuals belong to a group of one: themselves alone. Everyone feels different and unique; many feel misunderstood or alienated; most feel they belong to a group that is stereotyped and treated unfairly by the vicissitudes of the world. Perhaps this is the human condition (existentialists would say so), and cultural insensitivity stems from this alienation. In practical effect, everyone is different—special—and is hurt by the effects of cultural insensitivity. Putting the cosmic philosophy aside, however, people in a working environment have to find a way to mutually achieve their goals with a minimum of stress and conflict. A proactive approach to cultural sensitivity that strives to understand human differences before they become problems is probably the best model we have for addressing and managing group differences. Never before in the history of the world has a culture striven so hard to create high ideals and then live up to them in its laws and social behaviors as has America. The price of this effort is constant struggle, because the roots of prejudice are deep. Your efforts to be a part of the solution, rather than standing back and remaining silent, are necessary to make these ideals realities.

# Getting to Know Someone

*Instructions:* *Have you ever gotten to know and grown to respect someone who was of a different cultural group than your own? Have this person in mind as you reread the section in this chapter on awareness, acceptance, and respect. Then, in the space below compose a short essay in which you relate how you went through these three stages with that person. Give specific examples of things that happened in each of the three stages. Be prepared to share this experience with others.*

## EXERCISE 36

# Recognizing Challenges and Finding Solutions

*Instructions: From the exercise in this chapter on types of special groups, select a fairly specific special group that is different from your own. Try to imagine what it would be like to be a member of this group. In the worksheet below, do the following analysis:*

*Step 1. Identify the special problems that a member of this group faces that are different from yours. Be as thorough as you can in considering the challenges and difficulties that this person has to face as a student at your school.*

*Step 2. Identify the real resources on your campus (if there are any) to help this person contend with these challenges and problems. Do some research into these special services or programs available for members of this special group.*

*Step 3. Develop some ideas for better solutions than the ones that already exist. Working with a partner, brainstorm ideas for how the problems in Step 1 could be better met on your campus.*

Special group under consideration:

1. Special problems of a person in this group:

2. Resources for solutions on this campus:




3. Ideas for more solutions:

# Identifying Cultural Bias

*Instructions: For each of the following comments that you might overhear in a campus situation, identify the lack of sensitivity (if any) in the statement and the reasons you think it is insensitive. Also write a response you would make if you were in this situation and being addressed.*

1. "You have a lot of analytical aptitude for a woman. You'll do well in this department."

2. "I've got this great Mexican joke. I hope nobody minds."

3. "Mildred, why don't you give us the feminist perspective on this since you seem to have those leanings."

4. "Don't you think sculpture would be a bit difficult as a major for someone with your disability?" (to a student with limited mobility in a wheelchair)

5. "You're from Ridgemont High? No wonder you're having trouble in math. Kids from there never have good background skills in math."

6. "This class will require that you attend an additional review session every Wednesday night and take five weekend field trips if you are serious about passing." (to a single mother with two young children)

7. "I was particularly looking for a man as a research assistant, since there will be some heavy lifting of crates involved in the lab work." (to a woman)

# 11

## "What am I going to do when I get out of here?"

Some students have a clear career plan upon entering college. They know exactly what they want to do when they graduate, and they understand which college classes and experiences will contribute to that goal. They are the exception, however. Most college students enter school with only vague ideas of where their education will lead them. They know that a college degree will be invaluable for opening doors and creating opportunities for them, but they have no clear picture yet of what they will do, or even what they want to do, once out of school.

Such lack of clarity is a good thing in the early years of college. It is fine to be flexible and willing to explore. Many possibilities will emerge that you never knew even existed. It is dangerous, however, to drift too long and to spend no time on thinking about future career needs. It is unfortunate if you graduate from school and have made no career plans—no job prospects, no idea of where to look for a job, no awareness of the skills and abilities you have to offer, no idea of the kinds of jobs available, no job search skills, and no clear sense of what you want to do. This leads to a kind of career desperation that results in people taking the first available job with no plan for where it will lead them, whether they are best suited for it, or whether they will be satisfied with it.

This chapter will introduce you to the steps of career planning and the activities you should begin doing to ensure that your college education prepares you for a satisfying career. It is never too early to begin career planning, and you can start at any stage of career readiness. Even if you have returned to college after working for several years, you may not be aware of all the possibilities that are available. A wonderful, satisfying job is out there waiting for you. But you should start now to make that possibility a reality. Your task is to develop your skills, determine what you have to offer, and discover the best opportunity to use your skills.

## The Importance of Career Planning

At the beginning of their college careers, many college students think that things will take care of themselves and that all concerns about careers will be solved magically once the degree is in hand. That kind of thinking leads to many a sleepless night the summer after graduation. Knowledge about career possibilities, your analysis of your own interests, the development of skills and abilities to make you an attractive applicant, and the building of professional contacts to help you into the job market take time—lots of it! You need to begin planning and working now to make a career emerge.

There are two basic approaches to career planning: the job-oriented and you-oriented approaches. The **job-oriented approach** is what uninformed job seekers do. When they are ready for a job, they open the newspaper, and scan the want ads, looking for THE JOB. If they are lucky, they might find an opening. And if they are extremely lucky, they might beat out the hundred other applicants who also have applied for that job. But odds are not high in the job-seekers' advantage. There are not a lot of attractive jobs listed in the want ads, and the attractive ones have many applicants competing for the few openings.

In contrast to this dismal picture, the **you-oriented approach** to career planning starts with you: your interests, your skills, your knowledge, your ability to develop the skills and experience that employers will want, and your confidence that you know what you want, where it is located, and how to go about getting it. This approach makes job seeking much less stressful and much more successful. The techniques described in this chapter are based on the you-oriented approach, though they can be applied to the job-oriented approach as well. Starting with a you-orientation, however, will lead to a much more systematic and thorough career plan.

The following issues have to be addressed, generally in the order in which they are presented, for you to get a complete picture of you and the job market. You may have already done some planning in some areas. If so, you should try to verify your ideas with a knowledgeable job counselor to make sure you have not overlooked any possibilities. If you are a novice in career planning, you should begin at the top and work through the list of activities, being as thorough as possible. It is good to check in with a career counselor occasionally just to get a sounding board for your ideas and to see if the counselor has any suggestions. Your school probably has a career planning office whose job is to help you in these career activities. Instructors who are concerned about student job placement and professional friends also make effective career counselors. Take advantage of these resources and assistance as you gather the information you need.

1. **Determine your interests.** The most difficult, but most important, first step is to determine your own career interests. The biggest complaint, and the biggest obstacle to career planning, for college students is, "I don't know what I want to do." As you do the following career activities and gather information, you will begin to get some ideas about what you might like to do in the future. You must start somewhere, however, or this attitude will be a permanent barrier preventing you from going any further in the career planning process. The best way to determine your career interests is to take vocational tests. Your local career center will have several of these available. The counselors there will discuss the results with you. Several career planning books, such as Richard Bolles' *What Color Is Your Parachute?*, include career interest tests that you can take on your own. Exercise 38 at the end of this chapter is a simple career interest diagnostic activity that may give you some ideas of your internal motivations for a career. It is important to start with your own personality and the interests that emerge from it, because that will be the foundation for satisfaction in a career. You should pick a career area consistent with your values, personal style, and philosophy. Good diagnostic tools will help you determine these.

2. **Determine your skills and abilities.** Closely related to interests are the job-related skills you have developed. They are related because people gain skills in the areas that interest them. For example, if you like to play basketball, you probably have developed basketball skills. If you do not like to play basketball, you probably have not developed those skills. The same is true in any

activity. Identifying related interests and skills and abilities will show you how much you have already set yourself on a career path. You just may not be aware of it. Career centers have skills diagnostic tests that will give you information about the skills and abilities you have already attained. Generally, the best career strategy is to build upon your strengths, not to branch off in a totally new direction. Skills diagnostic tests will help you understand where your skills lie.

3. **Research general career options.** Once you have determined your interests and skills, you should begin to see how those apply to general career areas. For example, if your interests are "working with people" and "helping" and you have developed skills in "communication" and "problem-solving," you probably will be interested in one of the helping professions: counseling, teaching, or therapy. If your interests are in "making money" and "business" and you have abilities in "math" and "analytical skills," some business-related career area, such as accounting or finance, might be best for you. Within any general career area will be hundreds of possible job titles that combine interests and skills in unusual ways. You should start with the general area and work to the more specific job to find the position that is best aligned with your own needs. You may also have several conflicting sets of interests and skills. Work through each set to determine which is more appropriate for you. As you gather information, you will be better able to see which will be best for you.

4. **Explore specific job titles.** Having found a general career area that seems in line with your interests and skills, you need to explore the specific job possibilities in that area. The job description listed in a book is quite different from reality. You can start by doing library research, but you also should visit job sites, talk to people who actually work at those jobs, and get experience in specific job areas to see if the reality fits your perceptions. Many people go all the way through a college degree program thinking they are going to pursue a specific career, and their first week on the job after graduation is a rude awakening to how much they really do not like this kind of employment. Do not let this happen to you. Know what you are getting into by doing research in advance.

5. **Get experience.** One of the best ways to do research is to get actual work experience in a specific job. Experience is also one of your best qualifications in helping you get a job you want. Whenever possible, get actual experience in job areas you are considering through summer employment, internships, cooperative education, part-time employment, volunteer work, or class projects. Career-related jobs may not pay as much as unrelated employment, but consider the value of the experience, professional contacts, and knowledge you are gaining. They may be worth the sacrifice.

6. **Develop career-related skills.** Once you have determined the specific type of job you want to pursue, analyze it for the specific skills used in that job. Your selection of a major in college, optional courses, extracurricular activities, and additional skills development should be targeted toward providing you with the skills you will need in the future. These skills will make you more attractive as an applicant as well.

7. **Develop professional contacts.** One of the underlying secrets of getting a good job and advancing in a career is the matter of **networking**—cultivating contacts you know. As a student, you will have many opportunities to meet people in the job market through student organizations, professional associations, career-related activities, research, and employment experience. It is easy to let this opportunity slide by, however, because it takes a great deal of effort and courage to meet strangers. They are your best inroad to the career you want, however, and most of them want to meet you or they would not attend such meetings in the first place. Get to know people in your chosen field. They will be invaluable resources for information, advice, and job leads.

8. **Develop job search skills.** The most nerve-wracking part of career planning is the process of applying and interviewing for a job. To do these activities successfully and confidently, you need to master the specific skills of resume writing, application letter writing, interviewing, and finding job openings. Many career centers offer workshops in these skills, and many good books are available for you to study on your own. Some colleges offer courses in job search skills. Practice these skills to become proficient. Do not wait until the actual event to start practicing.

9. **Begin the job search.** Your search for a position should begin even while you are in school. Do not wait until after graduation to begin looking. It usually takes several months to go through the entire process of looking, finding, applying, interviewing, and accepting. During your last year in school, you can begin the process by letting potential employers know you will be available soon. If you have developed a strong professional network, people will be asking you when you are available. If you have done good research, met professional contacts, and gained experience in your chosen career area, you already should be aware of job openings. Applying for a position will be a natural step, not an awesome challenge.

## The Four-Year Career Plan

Your career planning should begin your first year in college and continue through each year. By steadily working at it, you will save yourself from falling victim to career desperation the last few months of your senior year. The following suggestions illustrate the various steps you can take each year to apply the career planning techniques discussed above. The sooner you start, the more time you will have for thorough research and to change your mind if you decide a certain path is not right for you.

**First year.** This year should be spent settling in and learning to enjoy the college experience, but you also can begin doing preliminary career planning and investigating.

- Visit the career center and complete interest and skills diagnostic tests. These tests will give you general guidelines for careers, majors, and courses to consider taking while in college.
- Begin researching the career options indicated in your diagnostic test results. If your interests and skills seem to be pointing you in a certain direction, do library and field research to see what those career areas are generally like and the kinds of specific jobs available there.
- Notice which classes you enjoy and the career-related skills you seem best at. Talk with instructors about career options related to classes you are taking.
- Get a feel for the career area that seems to fit you best. Talk with people you know and trust about career areas that might be right for you.

**Second year.** During your sophomore year you should begin to get more specific about career areas or specific jobs you will target as real job possibilities.

- Explore possible career areas by investigating them thoroughly. Do library research about specific industries, companies, or job titles. Gather information from career counselors about specific job descriptions and career areas that interest you.
- Get to know the "in's and out's" of what real jobs are actually like if you've never had one. Get a feel for the kind of job you want by interviewing people who actually perform these jobs. Consider using summer and part-time employment to help you gain experience and information in areas you want to explore.
- Get involved in extracurricular activities at school. Participation in these organizations and events will give you the opportunity to develop skills and make professional contacts that will be useful in the future.
- If nothing seems to be coming into focus for you, talk to career counselors about additional vocational testing to help clarify your interests and skills.

**Third year.** Generally, most students select a major and focus their college studies during their third year. Your choice of major and curriculum should be aligned with the career directions you uncovered in the first two years.

- Talk with instructors in your major area about career possibilities. Instructors in your major area should be able to give you specific details about careers and provide referrals for professional people to interview. Use class projects and assignments in your major classes to gather career-related information.
- Get involved in professional organizations to begin developing your career network. Many useful professional contacts can be made in these organizations, and you can demonstrate your abilities by taking leadership roles in them.
- Consider internships and cooperative education experience that will get you into the workplace to do firsthand research on specific jobs.
- Continue your research of specific positions with information-gathering interviews. Talk with people who actually are working in positions that interest you. Their insights will be extremely valuable.

**Fourth year.** The last year of school is usually a hectic one, but you should be at the stage in your career planning when you can begin the job search.

- Have a fairly clear idea of the job you want, the type of company in which you want to work, the region of the country in which you want to live, and additional schooling or training you will need to qualify for the job.
- Take workshops or courses that develop your job-search skills in writing resumes and letters and in interviewing. Prepare your resume and practice your interviewing skills.
- Do research on specific companies to which you want to apply. Conduct library research and information-gathering interviews to give you an inside look into the companies you have targeted as likely employers. The more you know, the more attractive you will be as an applicant.
- Sign up for on-campus interviews that you can use for placement. Contact your career or placement service for details of this service.
- Arrange your own preliminary employment interviews with possible employers off campus. Not all good employers will interview on campus. Potential employers will respect your assertiveness and forethought if you do your own advance interviewing and planning off campus.

By the time you graduate, you should have a precise picture of where you want to work and how to apply for the position.

As you can see, many activities contribute to a thorough career plan. Leaving all of them for the last year means that many of them will not get done. This lack of preparation limits your knowledge of the opportunities that could be available to you and weakens your qualifications as an applicant for the jobs to which you do apply. Start early and be ahead of the crowd to get the greatest advantage from these techniques.

## The Information-Gathering Interview

One of the best tools for doing research and making professional contacts is the **information-gathering interview.** This is a simple request to interview someone who has information that can help you in making your own career decisions. You use it to interview instructors, counselors, or business contacts. People in business are usually willing to talk with students who are interested in pursuing the same career they have chosen. You may get a few refusals because of time pressures, but most business people are flattered by your interest. What you propose as a 20-minute interview often stretches to an hour or more. These people also become contacts who then can lead you to other resources or opportunities to explore your field of interest.

You can use the information-gathering interview to gain preliminary information about a career field, to get an overview of a company or an industry, or to do an in-depth analysis of a specific position. Likewise, you can use the interview to discover job openings, to get referrals that will extend your professional network, or to gather information that will help you in the application process.

The information-gathering interview requires thorough preparation to get the maximum benefit from the short time you have with the person you are visiting. The following steps will help you prepare for these interviews.

1. **Determine your best expert sources.** To get the best information, you need to select the most knowledgeable and helpful people. You can get names of people to interview from instructors, career counselors, industry directories, and people you already know in the area of your interests. Once you get the first interview, you can always ask for referrals to other people to interview. This is the best way to extend your network and meet more people in your area of interest.

2. **Do your homework.** To utilize your time effectively, determine exactly the kind of information you are looking for and do as much preliminary background research as possible before interviewing the expert. Know as much as you can so you do not cover elementary information with the expert that you could have found on your own.

3. **Prepare your questions in advance.** Plan a general outline of questions and refer to it during the interview so you cover all the areas you want to explore. Be ready to stray from the

planned outline if the interview goes in helpful, but unexpected, directions. Your outline will help you stay on track and stay within the time limits you ask for when you set up the interview.

4. **Set up the interview.** The easiest way to make contact with someone you do not know already is to have a mutual acquaintance refer you. People are much more willing to talk to friends of friends than to strangers. If you do not have a referral, you can introduce yourself and your purpose through a letter. Contact also can be made by means of a telephone call. Many people will want to do the interview immediately over the phone when you call, but it is best to ask to see them face-to-face so you get to know them personally.

5. **Conduct the interview.** Once you have arranged and shown up for the interview, the following areas are typically covered in career-related information-gathering interviews:

- Open the conversation with remarks about whom you know in common, your purpose, the general areas you want to cover in the interview, and a brief introduction of yourself.

- Investigate job responsibilities with questions about what specific tasks are involved in a particular job, the skills it takes to do this job, the training a person needs to do a job, and the advantages and disadvantages of this job.

- Investigate the interviewee's company by asking about how it is different from or similar to other companies in the same industry, what it is like to work for this particular company, and new developments within the company.

- Investigate an industry by asking questions related to industry trends, new products or developments on the horizon, and new career possibilities in this field.

- Get advice by asking for recommendations about courses you should take, extracurricular activities you should do, additional skills you should gain while in college, or how you should go about preparing yourself for a career in this field.

- Get to know the person better by asking about his opinions and experiences within this company and doing this job.

- Ask for referrals to other people within this company or industry whom you might talk to for more information.

When people take time to help you with career information, you should respond with professional courtesy by offering to take them to lunch, giving them a small gift of thanks, or writing a note expressing your appreciation. The people you interview probably will become your professional colleagues in future years, so it is worthwhile to establish your credibility now as a well-prepared, organized, and considerate person.

## Closing Thoughts

An added benefit of learning career planning and job search skills is that they will last you through your whole life. You will use the same processes of self-analysis, research, networking, interviewing, and job search skills continually as you work your way up the career ladder of your chosen field. Few people stay in the same job forever. You should expect to change jobs, companies, industries, or even careers several times in your working life. If you have developed good career planning skills the first time, you will have them ready to use when you need them later. Because work is such an important part of American culture, you will also have skills with which to help others make important career decisions.

# Identifying Your Career Interests and Skills

*Instructions:* *Complete the following questions to give you some insight into possible career areas that fit your unique interests and skills. Compare these to vocational diagnostic tests you take at the career center at your school.*

1. If you were to have a day totally free of responsibilities, what would you do? What activities are most enjoyable for you?

2. If you were to win a lottery suddenly and have a million dollars a year for the rest of your life (thus not having to work for a living), what would you do with your time? What activities would you use to fill your years of free time?

3. What aspect of life would you like to make some contribution to? If you could become an world-renowned expert in some field, what would you choose?

4. As a child, did you ever have secret ambitions to "be something" but the idea got lost or dropped along the way? What were some of these early ambitions?

5. Have you unconsciously chosen not to pursue certain careers because of reasons such as "you can't make a living doing that" or "it just wouldn't work out?" What were some of these career areas?

6. If you had to find a job tomorrow to support yourself, what are you qualified to do? List the skills you have that would help you do that job.

7. Which subjects in school do you enjoy, are best at, or come most easily to you?

8. Have you made a specific career choice? If so, what is it, and what skills do you have in that area? If not, what have people who know you well said you should consider as a career? Why?

# Researching a Job Title

*Instructions:* *Select a specific job title about which you would like to know more and that may be of interest to you as a possible future career area. See if your career center has information on specific job descriptions. Also look in the* Dictionary of Occupational Titles *in your library to gather information about this specific job. Record your findings below.*

Job title researched:

Description of job responsibilities:

Skills needed to perform this job:

Personality traits required to perform this job well:

Companies in which this job is performed (potential employers):

Based on the above information, summarize how this job is consistent or not with your interests, skills, and personality traits:

# Interviewing for Career Information

*Instructions:* *Following the instructions for conducting an information-gathering interview presented in this chapter, arrange a meeting with someone who is employed in a job about which you would like to learn. Take notes during the interview, and summarize the information you received in the worksheet below.*

Person interviewed:

Job title:

Company worked for:

How you selected this person to interview:

Purpose of the interview:

Questions you asked:

Summary of information you gathered:

Was the interview valuable to you and your career planning? If so, how? If not, what problems should you avoid in your next career interview?

# Final Thoughts

This book has addressed 11 common questions that the average college student asks sometime in his or her career. These areas do not exhaust the challenges a new student faces, however. Many other topics could have been included in this book.

To review, this book has covered the 10 important skill areas of:

1. goal-setting skills
2. decision-making and time management skills
3. study skills
4. test-taking skills
5. research skills
6. communication skills
7. faculty–student relationship skills
8. problem-solving and curriculum-planning skills
9. career-planning skills
10. intercultural sensitivity skills

Now that you have some experience as a college student, what other problem areas have you encountered or seen other students encounter? What other kinds of skills would be useful for first-year students to learn? In the space below, list some other kinds of problem situations that college students might face during their first year on campus:

If you were writing this book, you might have chosen to include some of these topics. (That might not be such a bad idea. Have you ever considered writing a book based on the solutions you have found for problems you have confronted as a student? That is all this book has done.) In fact, other writers of books similar to this one have included chapters on the following problems and solutions:

| | |
|---|---|
| alcohol abuse | making new friends |
| drug abuse | sexual intimacy |
| nutrition | health and wellness |
| stress management | community activism |
| interpersonal relations | child care |
| recreation and exercise | financial aid |
| weight control | commuting |
| word processing | computer skills |

No book can cover all possible topics. One of the underlying purposes of this book, however, has been to train you in finding your own solutions. This is done through the problem-solving process as it applies to college life. This process for analyzing problems and finding solutions was introduced earlier. The basic steps in the problem-solving process are:

1. Becoming aware of problems or potential problem areas.
2. Searching for resources to find solutions.
3. Selecting the best solution available.
4. Applying and testing the solution to see if it works.

In the various chapters in this book, I have attempted to encourage the skills you will need in the four stages of problem solving. Goal setting is necessary to know when a problem is important enough to you to do something about it. Time management, studying, and test taking are common problem areas that all students face. Research skills are necessary for finding solutions that others have found workable. Communication skills are needed to involve others in your search for the best solution. Faculty relationships, curriculum and career planning, finances, and intercultural sensitivity are all resource areas that can be helpful to you in finding solutions and avoiding problems while attending school. Thus, the underlying message of every chapter has been the problem-solving process:

1. What is the problem, and why is it a problem?
2. Where can you go to find possible solutions?
3. What techniques does the solution entail?
4. How do you apply these techniques and make them work for you?

This book started with the question, "What is success?" College success is the feeling of accomplishment and satisfaction you have about your role as a student. It is not grades, or good times, or winning awards (though those things may be symbolic of some larger value you might have). In the long run, success will be how well you decide for yourself about your own goals and how well you work toward achieving them.

To that end, this book has covered skills that are necessary in the problem-solving process. You will need many other skills, because many other problem situations are waiting for you in the future. This book has been written to help prepare you to meet those challenges. The learning process never stops. During each stage of your life, you will be confronted with the same kinds of challenges that you met when you first came to college: new responsibilities, new tasks, new people, new opportunities. The skills you learn as a college student are the same skills you will need in these future stages of your life.

How well have you learned these skills? Return to Exercise 2, "Assessing Your Success Skills," and complete the rating form again. Compare your end-of-term score to your beginning-of-term score. Have you improved? What are the areas you still need to develop? Are you convinced that these skills are useful and necessary to your success?

If you have begun to improve, you will see the need to continue your improvement. New situations will require new adaptations. With a solid foundation, you will have the skills and confidence to succeed. I hope that this course has been helpful in giving you those building blocks to success. Good luck in your future careers.

# Index